CARRIE MAE WEEMS
RECENT WORK, 1992–1998

CARRIE MAE WEEMS

RECENT WORK, 1992–1998

WITH ESSAYS BY
THOMAS PICHÉ, JR., AND THELMA GOLDEN

GEORGE BRAZILLER PUBLISHER, NEW YORK
IN ASSOCIATION WITH EVERSON MUSEUM OF ART, SYRACUSE, NEW YORK

This publication was prepared on the occasion of the exhibition
"Carrie Mae Weems: Recent Work, 1992–1998" held at Everson Museum of Art
from September 26, 1998 to February 14, 1999, organized by Thomas Piché, Jr.

Carrie Mae Weems: Recent Work, 1992–1998 is made possible with funding from The Rosamond Gifford Charitable Corporation; the Central New York Community Foundation; public funds from the New York State Council on the Arts, a state agency; Lannan Foundation; The Peter Norton Family Foundation; Carrier Corporation; and the Chase Manhattan Foundation.

Copyright © 1998 by Everson Museum of Art

All rights reserved. No reproduction of this book in whole or in part, in any form or by any means may be made without written authorization of the copyright owner.

For information, please address the publisher:
George Braziller, Inc.
171 Madison Avenue
New York, NY 10016

Library of Congress Cataloging-in-Publication Data:
Weems, Carrie Mae, 1953–
    Carrie Mae Weems : recent work, 1992–1998 / with essays by Thomas Piché, Jr., and Thelma Golden.
    p.   cm.
    Prepared on the occasion of the exhibition held at Everson Museum of Art, Sept. 26, 1998–Feb. 14, 1999.
    Includes bibliographical references (p.).
    ISBN 0-8076-1444-0 (hardback)
    1. Photography, Artistic—Exhibitions. 2. Weems, Carrie Mae, 1953-   —Exhibitions.
I. Piché, Thomas.   II. Golden, Thelma.   III. Everson Museum of Art.   IV. Title.
TR647.W382   1998
779'.074747'66—dc21   98-44788
                                                                                         CIP

Designed by Rita Lascaro
Printed and bound in Italy by G. Canale & C.
First edition

TABLE OF CONTENTS

6   Foreword

7   Acknowledgments

9   Reading Carrie Mae Weems by Thomas Piché, Jr.

29   Some Thoughts on Carrie Mae Weems by Thelma Golden

35   Catalogue

136   Exhibition Checklist

140   Biography

146   Selected Bibliography

FOREWORD

During my many years in the museum field, I've rarely been as inspired by a body of artwork as I am by the diverse series of Carrie Mae Weems. Weems possesses a rare combination of critical insight and aesthetic understanding, which she uses to examine some of the most important concerns of our time. Her work invites us to consider issues that we often avoid because they are tough and contentious and require serious thought. Through her use of photographs, wall text, freely hanging banners, and sculpture, Weems creates environments where she is able to evoke both emotional and intellectual responses from viewers. In this way she involves us in a multilayered appreciation of installations that are themselves nuanced and multivalent. The Everson is truly proud and honored to be able to share this work with the public through this retrospective and catalogue.

For the central New York community, this exhibition represents a debut of sorts for Carrie Mae Weems, who has recently moved her home and studio to Syracuse. As this exhibition foretells, our artistic and cultural lives will certainly be the richer for her presence. We can all look forward to experiencing the continued results of her enormous energy and talent.

I'd like to commend Thomas Piché, Jr., the Everson's senior curator, for the commitment he made to this project. Tom dedicated a considerable amount of energy and talent to organizing this show and catalogue during the past two years. His relationship with Weems and the results of their collaboration demonstrate another kind of art—the art of curatorship.

The critical social engagement that Weems's work represents calls for serious dialogue with our audiences through educational programming. Thanks to the generous grants from The Rosamond Gifford Charitable Corporation, the Central New York Community Foundation, the New York State Council on the Arts, The Peter Norton Family Foundation, the Lannan Foundation, and Carrier Corporation, we are able to offer the central New York community, and anyone else who'll make the trip, an unprecedented array of programming that is certain to enhance our experience of Weems's work. Thanks to you all.

SANDRA TROP, Director
Everson Museum of Art

ACKNOWLEDGMENTS

Throughout the two years of planning, research, and organization of "Carrie Mae Weems: Recent Work, 1992–1998," I have been fortunate to have had the assistance, encouragement, and collaboration of a number of individuals. I'd like to thank them here.

The process of putting this show together has been a personally enriching one and was largely made so because of the generosity of Carrie Mae Weems. Weems has been unselfish in discussions concerning her many series and in making her work accessible to me during studio visits and numerous discussions in Syracuse and elsewhere. Her enthusiasm for this project has been unflagging, and we are all indebted to her for her willingness to share her work with the Everson.

My appreciation is also extended to Thelma Golden for the contribution of her insightful essay. The production of this handsome catalogue was nurtured and shepherded by George Braziller and Mary Taveras at George Braziller, Inc.; thank you both. Scott Catto at P.P.O.W. was enormously and unwaveringly helpful with concerns large and small. Thank you Scott. Thanks also to Penny Pilkington and Wendy Olsoff at the gallery for their support. The loan of the series *From Here I Saw What Happened and I Cried* was crucial to the show, and I am grateful to Peter Galassi, Virginia Dodier, and Alexia Hughes at the Museum of Modern Art for allowing the series to travel to the Everson. Thanks also to Susan Cahan, at The Peter Norton Family Foundation, and to Jenée Misraje and Kathleen Merril, at the Lannan Foundation, for their generous support of this project.

I'd especially like to thank my colleagues at the Everson. It is only because of their remarkable teamwork that any show or catalogue ever comes to fruition. Throughout the long process of financial planning, research, interpretation, and installation, I have been fortunate for their encouragement, advice, and critical input: Director Sandra Trop, Director of Development Kristine Waelder, Curator of Education Marion Wilson, Coordinator of School Programs Pam McLaughlin, Registrar Michael Flanagan, Public Information Officer Katherine Blodgett, Building Manager Bill Waelder, and the installation crew— Manny Burgos and Mark Stanley. My sincerest thanks to you all. Finally, my warm appreciation is extended to Craig Watters, whose insights, analyses, patience, and exhortations were invaluable during the course of the project.

THOMAS PICHÉ, Jr., Senior Curator
Everson Museum of Art

READING CARRIE MAE WEEMS

Carrie Mae Weems pursues the arts as a cultural worker. As an artist committed to radical social change, she has created artwork that incisively examines, among other subjects, issues of race and racism, class and classism, gender and sexism. Although primarily known as a photographer, in the course of her twenty-year career, Weems has also employed written texts, banners, commemorative plates, sound, and sculpture. These various media have been combined to create a rich array of documentary series, still lifes, narrative tableaux, and installation pieces. Throughout her work, Weems's understated goal has been to "describe simply and directly those aspects of American culture in need of deeper illumination."[1]

Although Weems has been making artwork since 1978, this essay will consider at some length five works that have been created since 1992, including the *Sea Islands Series* (1991–92), the *Africa Series* (1993), *From Here I Saw What Happened and I Cried* (1995–96), *Who What When Where,* and *Ritual & Revolution* (both from 1998). In these series, Weems leads us to consider and to share what we know about our collective folkways, about life at the beginning of time, and about the culture of slavery; she involves us in questioning whether art making has the ability to impact society; she leaves us with a haunting and ephemeral ode to history. Although each of these series is a discrete work in itself, with a particular look, character, and inspiration, each shares and compounds the concerns that the artist has engaged from the beginning: "I want to make things that are beautiful, seductive, formally challenging and culturally meaningful," she states. "I'm also committed to radical social change.... Any form of human injustice moves me deeply...the battle against all forms of oppression keeps me going and keeps me focused."[2]

Carrie Mae Weems is a wanderer. Born in Portland, Oregon, in 1953 into a black working-class family, she has moved from the West Coast of the United States to islands off its East Coast; has journeyed to the Slave Coast of Africa and to its interior savannas and ancient cities; and to the Russian steppes and to the cities associated with the October Revolution. In her intellectual travels, Weems has looked high and low, encountering in her explorations a broad range of philosophers, artists, and writers. She has drawn on the folklore of the rural American South, the writings of revolutionaries both current and past, the blues, art history, and cultural theorists. She has had encounters with Karl Marx, Bessie Smith, Vladimir Tatlin, Zora Neale Hurston, and Roy DeCarava. The diverse bodies of work Weems has produced since 1978 are the result of these physical and intellectual journeys.

Carrie Mae Weems is an image maker. She was given her first camera by a friend in 1971 and used it to document the activities of the political groups she was associated with in the San Francisco Bay area—general photographs of antiwar demonstrations, feminist marches, and left-wing political events. By her own recollection, within six months of her first photograph she began to seek out and pay attention to the work of professional documentary photographers, including Robert Frank, Henri Cartier-Bresson, and, especially, Roy DeCarava. Later, after having already developed an engaged eye and an understanding of the camera as a social tool, she pursued a formal education in photography, receiving a BFA from the California Institute of the Arts and an MFA from the University of California at San Diego.

As a result of these early experiences and influences, Weems adopted a documentary style of photography, adapted to her particular interests, that she continues to use. She has asserted that "photography can still be used to champion activism [and] as a powerful weapon toward instituting political and cultural change."[3] With those ends in mind, Weems plays with the idea of documentary photography, subverting, even while appropriating, the authority of the genre; reconfiguring its format to better express her subjects' iconic, metaphoric, or symbolic value, and whatever discourse she chooses to pursue.

Weems's photographs are characteristically square in shape, partly a function of the two-and-one-quarter-inch camera format she prefers. Economy of form and spareness of setting are hallmarks of Weems's mature style. They typically employ a truncated foreground space that opens onto subjects that are shot in a straightforward, head-on manner. For Weems this compositional style is metaphoric for confronting head-on the material of the world.[4] She also likes a Rolleiflex lens because it gives clarity to the photographic subject but yields a slightly soft focus that implies a sense of past time—something a little old, but still contemporary. She wants photographs that have an element of lived texture, rather than a pristine print; she's not interested in eliminating the grain, and in her most recent work this aspect is exaggerated for metaphoric intent.

Weems first received critical attention for her exhibition "Family Pictures and Stories" in 1984. This series combined photographs, text, and the spoken word, focusing on the construction of a family narrative. It was here that she first revealed the technical and critical strategies that continue to inform much of her work: the creation of visual and acoustic environments where the viewer is asked to join in the creation of a shared experience of acknowledgment, recognition, and change. Her sustained interest in and study of folklore and oral traditions led to the *Ain't Jokin* series of 1987. Here Weems tackled racialized humor and the use of stereotypes in our culture. In the *Kitchen Table* series of 1990, Weems directed her gaze at the subject of female representation, human relationships, and the overarching concerns of race and class. Using herself as the protagonist, Weems created a series of tableaux vivants combined with extended texts that look inside and outside the imagined world of her photographs. In 1991, she mounted a fully active environment entitled *And 22 Million Very Tired and Very Angry People,* where ceiling-hung, text-laden banners joined wall-mounted photographs and emblematic captions. Directly addressing class and gender issues, it was her first series not to concentrate on photographic portraits and the first to speak distinctly of the broad spectrum of revolutionaries, theorists, and social activists who inform her work.

The topic of race has been central to most discussions concerning the work of Carrie Mae Weems. A survey of her diverse series from the past twenty years would seem to support the notion that race and representation are key areas of investigation for the artist. Since her earliest series, *Family Pictures and Stories,* she has set out "to refigure and reintroduce the black subject to ourselves." She has examined subjects that are ostensibly linked to issues encircling African-American culture, including personal and cultural history, Africa, and traces of the diaspora in the black Atlantic.[5] However, in both published interviews and private conversation, Weems expresses her frustration with the narrow focus of racialized critiques: "[O]ne of the things that I was thinking about was whether it might be possible to use black subjects to represent universal concerns.... Yet when I do that, it's not understood in that way. Folks refuse to identify with the concerns black people express which take us beyond race...."[6]

Weems has insisted on the black subject being treated as part of the fabric of the larger society. What affects blacks, affects all. What they affect has ramifications in other communities. She holds that her use of the black subject is not self-referential, that the black subject can speak for more than itself, that it can speak across race and class lines to issues of isolated identity; to how we participate in the construction of our lives and are accomplices to our social situations; and to other concerns that affect all humankind. As bell hooks reminds us, "[Weems's] work encourages us not to see the black subject through the totalizing lens of race...she consistently invites us to engage the black subject in ways that call attention to the specificity of race...without privileging it as the only relevant category of analysis."[7] By examining the myths, the stereotypes, and the popular and media sources that frame information about black people, Weems sets out to explore the more encompassing issues of power relationships, gender, identity, and class, as well as race.

"Let me simply say that my primary concern in art, as in politics, is with the status and place of Afro-Americans in our country."[8] When asked recently if she still was in agreement with this statement made in 1989, Weems responded:

> The thing I'm most interested in at this moment is the complexity of human experience and relationships, be they African American or otherwise. When I first started making photographs, I was very aware that there were very few pictures of African Americans and that they always stood for themselves. My sense was that images of white people could speak about universal concerns. I wanted to use images of blacks in the same way, so that representations of blacks and materials associated with blacks could stand for more than themselves and for more than a problem, that they could speak about the human condition. But I've come to realize that the way blacks are represented in our culture makes it almost impossible to get that point across. So, I'm now asking the questions in a different way. Notions of black representation are still very important to me, and will always be a concern. In fact, it is now absolutely my assumption that people of color do speak to something bigger than themselves. I assume that that is just fine, whether writers and critics get it or not—it's not my problem. If they don't get it then my work is misunderstood and racialized.

As a white middle-class male, I come to Weems's work with experiences and perceptions that encourage me to focus on the notions encircling blackness that are found there. In conversations with colleagues, the connection of Weems's work to black representation is an apparently logical link we struggle to place in perspective. Much of the critical discourse that centers on Weems's various series pays scant attention to issues of the politics of gender, class, and power, and instead focuses on black subjectivity. Does this lack of accord between the artist's intention and her audience's perception exist because, as bell hooks avows, "we lack a critical language to talk about contemporary radical subjectivity"?[9] And is it that even those with the grounding in a black analytical tradition refuse to include "regimes of visuality" (including black visual art, art criticism, and artists) in their critical discourse, as has been suggested by Michele Wallace?[10] Or could it be that the social construction of understanding vis-à-vis blacks and their visual representation is so steeped in racist history as to obviate any reading but one that is racialized?

As my colleague Craig Watters has pointed out, "We can't avoid our history. Visually we have had almost four hundred years of images that have depicted black people in a certain way to accomplish certain goals. Historically, black people were imaged as African exotics, slaves, and, later, as animalistic buffoons, criminals, layabouts, sex dogs, and so forth. These images circulated among Americans in newspapers, journals, cartoon strips, books, movies, magazines, and television. Historically, they can't be undone, unread, or erased."[11]

Certainly, Weems understands this. A central component of her art-making strategy is a process of deconstruction, whereby the conventions that bind us to stereotypic and conventional readings of images of blacks are systematically challenged. As bell hooks puts it, "Carrie Mae Weems's photoworks create a cartography of experience wherein race, gender, and class identity converge, fuse, and mix so as to disrupt and deconstruct simple notions of subjectivity."[12] One way that Weems has addressed this is to become actively engaged in redressing the gaps and spaces in the history of the marginalized, to restore subjugated knowledge, and to provide a place for the unrecorded voices of the working class, of enslaved Africans, women, and the ghosts of the oppressed worldwide to be heard. Weems is involved with creative remembrance, with the reconstruction of emotional, personal accounts of the undocumented past. This, in itself, is an act of critical intervention and resistance. Henry Louis Gates, Jr., describes the origin of this need for remembrance and its outcome as follows: "Because of the experience of the diaspora, the fragments that contain the traces of a coherent system of order must be reassembled.... [T]o reassemble fragments, of course, is to engage in an act of speculation, to attempt to weave a fiction of origins and subgeneration. It is to render the implicit as explicit, and at times to imagine the whole from the part."[13]

And so Carrie Mae Weems is a storyteller. She enhances the episodic aspect of her photographs by employing text in her work; in fact, Weems's use of text to accompany her photographs is central to her art practice. She often constructs extended captions and full-blown narratives on separate panels to be placed within her photographic series. Sometimes the images themselves are silk-screened or inscribed with seemingly objective labels or sentences that have the quality of catchphrases. At some length, she has related the story of her family, folktales from slave days, and the story of Adam and Eve. In shorthand notation, she has told jokes, named names, and captioned capitalism. In this way she is able to create readings of her work that have the ring of truth associated with the documentary photo-essay or the social force implied by ancient myth.

One way of reading Weems's combination of photograph and text is through the lens of postmodern semiotics. If, as is commonly believed, a picture is worth a thousand words, that is so because of the uncertain connection between seeing and naming. It takes a thousand words, possibly more, to adequately describe the possibilities of meaning contained in a single image. As Andreas Hapkemeyer asserts in *photo text text photo:*

> Images are semanticized by virtue of the direct allocation of texts...texts, on the other hand, are unmistakably referentialized through the assignment of images.... [M]ore complex information, in an aesthetic sense, becomes possible. Text and image can complement one another.... The text may just as easily work against the message of the images... [or]...the text may inject a level of meaning not foreseen in the images by introducing a new theme.[14]

The use of text is also a way to alter the objectifying, dispassionate gaze of the camera, to restore the subjective voice, to reinsert a human dimension. Text is a way to direct meaning, to bring in the artist, not the artist as a mediator of universal truths, but the artist as auteur, directing the reading of a text with an authority that is derived from engagement with a point of view. Weems exploits the various results of combining image and text in her work in order to expand upon the layers and levels of meaning that her photoworks are able to embody.

Weems is not alone is her combination of image and text. Since the 1980s, the use of photograph and text has become the pre-eminent medium for politically motivated art. One need only think of the work of Gran Fury, Les Levine, Jenny Holzer, and Barbara Krueger. In modern art its use dates back to the work of the Cubists and was used to great effect by the Dadaists, Constructivists, and so on, into our own time. A consideration of the use of text in religious paintings of the early Renaissance or the hieroglyphics that accompanied Egyptian murals helps historicize the genre.

Another way to read Carrie Mae Weems, one that situates her practice outside of the Western tradition, can be illuminated by Henry Louis Gates's seminal analysis of the signifying tradition in African-American oral and written narratives.[15] Signifying—a way of showing off rhetorically—relies on metaphor, simile, pastiche, and a self-conscious mining of signifying's traditions in order to develop layered and nuanced meaning. This meaning is able to circulate in the specific work at hand as well as reference other works with which it shares kindred concerns. In this tradition, the text takes on a double-voiced character, combining the direct speech of an active participant and the third-person reportage of an omniscient observer. In this way, the narrative is able to yield a self-consciousness, a sense of self built on one's own terms, as well as to situate the self in the context of something larger than the individual. This characteristic holds a corrective mirror up to the double consciousness that W. E. B. Du Bois laments in *The Souls of Black Folk:* The African American "ever feels his twoness,—an American, a Negro; two souls, two thoughts, two unreconciled strivings; two warring ideals in one dark body.... The history of the American Negro is the history of this strife,—this longing to attain self-conscious manhood, to merge his double self into a better and truer self."[16]

In light of Gates's study, we are able to connect Weems's photoworks to a continuous legacy that stretches back to the slave narratives of the nineteenth century, reaching its modernist apogee in the writings of Zora Neale Hurston.[17] Weems has widely discussed her indebtedness to Hurston: "Finding my own artistic voice haunted me... And while scratching around for the sound of me.... I tripped over *Their Eyes Were Watching God* by Zora Neale Hurston.... I went to her watering-hole and drank long and deep, and there discovered my courage."[18] Of Hurston, Gates writes that she "realized a resonant and authentic narrative voice that echoes and aspires to the status of the impersonality, anonymity, and authority of the black vernacular tradition, a nameless, selfless tradition, at once collective and compelling, true somehow to the unwritten text of a common blackness. For Hurston, the search for a telling form of language, indeed the search for a black literary language itself, defines the search for the self."[19]

Through her warmly acknowledged connection to Hurston, Weems becomes heir to the tradition of oral narration that is found in classical African-American vernacular literature, what Gates calls "the speakerly text," that is, "a text whose rhetorical strategy is designed to represent an oral literary tradition."[20] Weems ties her work to the African-American literary tradition of signifying and creates a visual analogue, a sister system, that conforms to a storytelling structure. Weems's text is typically built on descriptive narrative, evocative apologues, and vernacular locutions. Rather than the text merely suggesting a reading of or meaning for the photographs, text and photographs are codependent and coequal, working together to create the layered meaning to be found in a particular work. In effect, Weems's photographs are double voiced, standing as visual images with multivalent meaning but functioning, as well, as semantic entities that give visual form to the rhetorical strategies found in the text. In this way, Weems creates a rich discursive alternative to Western modes of representation and a place to describe the voices that have been left out of dominant cultural practice. In her hands the black subject is given a voice through this use of signifying text and photography and becomes a speaking subject imbued with authority. As we shall see, Weems has also established within her oeuvre a trove of visual strategies, subjects, and textual tropes with their own traditions, historic echoes, and plain-speaking voices from which she samples, quotes, and appropriates in a way that mimics the self-referential character of signifying.

In her earliest work, *Family Pictures and Stories,* Weems explored in photographs and narrative her family's migration to Oregon from the southeastern United States. Her subsequent trip in 1991 to the coastal lowlands of the South was, thus, a journey made as descendent, as well as visitor and observer. In the *Sea Islands Series,* Weems confronts the legacy of slavery in the United States and the narrow notion that slavery had crushed the possibility of any cultural retention in blacks and that what culture there was imitated white customs.

The Sea Islands are a group of barrier islands that hug the coasts of South Carolina and Georgia. Since the seventeenth century, enslaved Africans and their descendants have constituted a majority population on the islands, living in relative isolation from white society. This population is commonly referred to as *Gullah,* a name that is related to the African place-name *Angola,* the region from which many of the area's original enslaved Africans came.[21] Historians, anthropologists, writers, and folklorists have long recognized the area as historically and culturally significant, particularly for the Gullahs' creation of a distinct, original African-American cultural form.

In the *Sea Islands Series,* Weems gives a voice to the character and culture of enslaved Africans and their descendents. She searches out what she terms "Africanisms," aspects of cultural retention that still exist there, three hundred years after the ancestors of these inhabitants made the journey from West Africa to America. In this series, Weems combines square-shaped, black-and-white photographs of landscapes, architecture, and tableaux of material culture with text panels that list African-derived words, folktales and aphorisms, and related narratives. She shows us the praise house, the slave quarters, and a smokehouse, landscapes of majestic trees hung with Spanish moss, a cemetery, and hubcaps flashing in sandy fields. Her texts, based on folklore, offer advice for daily life, for protecting the family, and preparations for birth and death. In each instance, links can be made between what on first glance appear to be not unusual scenes and material traces of the culture that was brought with the enslaved Africans. Henry Louis Gates, referring to a mounting body of research, attests that Africans took with them from their civilization aspects of their culture that were meaningful and that they chose not to forget: their music, their myths, their expressive institutional structures, their metaphysical systems of order, and their forms of performance. "The notion that the Middle Passage was so traumatic that it functioned to create in the African a tabula rasa of consciousness," he continues, "is as odd as it is a fiction, a fiction that has served several economic orders and their attendant ideologies."[22]

More than just capturing the humanity of the people and the place, Weems locates the sites of resistance and the places of refuge and spirituality, the sites of cultural fomentation and formation. Through the expression of the nature of the beliefs that have continued and how those beliefs shape the living of a life, Weems intends for us to see that most of us operate out of a similar system of beliefs. She asks us to locate in ourselves the folklore of our own families, to call upon our own histories in relation to the story that she shares with us and which at first may seem alien. By focusing on depictions of food, music, language, and religion, she also shows the sites of African influence on white America, the shared experience of us rather than the narrow notion of "other."[23]

On the day that Carrie Mae Weems returned home from the Sea Islands, she decided to go to Africa. She hoped to gain a personal, firsthand understanding of the way that Africa had impacted both her and America. She first traveled along the Slave Coast, the area where enslaved Africans were gathered in barracoons and from which they were deported to various destinations in the New World. "I immediately began photographing the vestiges of slavery: the slave ports, forts, castles along the coast of Ghana, Elmina and Cape Coast, and Ile de Gorée in Senegal."[24] She went there to get a feel for the great human tragedy and to explore this aspect of the historical past of which we are all a part.

The photographs that resulted from this early part of her journey are primarily architectural and move between being very descriptive and evocatively abstract. "It wasn't the experience I had expected, it was much more complicated than just claiming roots. I felt methodical and emotionally distant. I had to be efficient with my time and get the work done. I'd deal with the emotions later." After documenting the Slave Coast, Weems headed into the interior. She began talking with people, visiting rural villages. An encounter with a Hausa community, which decided that the village shrine was off-limits to her because she was a "white woman" (meaning, a foreigner) and whites had come before and had not kept their promises, came as something of an epiphany—you can't go home again. Her expectations continued to be challenged as she visited other villages along the Volta River and on into Mali and the cities of Timbuktu and Djenné. Here, away from the Slave Coast, Weems felt free to explore Africa in a broader way, to make associations, and to engage in a certain kind of play.

The resulting body of work, the *Africa Series,* was motivated by photographs of buildings and landscapes Weems took in and around Djenné, that oldest of African cities. These photographs of cultivated farm fields, dwellings with ladders, narrow and shadowed streets, functional granaries, and buttressed mosques are described in a straightforward manner: subjects are centered and balanced, filling the picture plane; the lighting enhances texture and volume. The gently focused black-and-white pictures have a timeless quality; typically without people or objects that might help to date them, they could be from the dawn of photography.

The text Weems writes to accompany the images has the feel of a creation myth. It deals with the relationship between the first woman and the first man and explores issues of desire, love, pleasure, pain, temptation, sin, betrayal, and power. The text is by turns playful and serious. It takes on the tone and cadence of religious oratory, it samples the poetry of the Song of Solomon and the narrative character of Zora Neale Hurston's *Their Eyes Were Watching God,* and mixes in snatches of everyday vernacular. The narrative clearly derives from the signifying tradition and the speakerly text, alternating between the asides of the outside observer and direct dialogue between Adam and Eve:

> So he came strumming the cora, bearing gifts of cowrie shells and cola nuts, blowing star-dust memories, dazzling her senses by recounting his powers:
>
> I can build a castle from a single grain of sand/I can make a ship sail on dry land/I can change a river into a raging fire/I can live forever if my soul desires.

The narrative plays off the sexuality that Weems found embedded in the stylistic features of the West African architecture, from the suggestively male towers of the Friday Mosque in Djenné[25] to the sensual female body form of granaries. In the gallery installation, she combines photographs and text in diptychs, triptychs, and polyptychs, and enhances the recital by placing actual West African objects—ladders and a chaise—in the center of the gallery. The gallery walls are lined with a wallpaper that features a motif of a female figure walking through dense foliage, derived from the endpapers of George Bernard Shaw's 1933 book *A Black Woman in Her Search for God*. Photographs are placed in corners; the entire space is activated.

A central component of the installation is a three-panel folding screen the artist designed using silkscreening and embroidery on fabric. The center panel bears the silk-screened image of a standing full-length female cloaked in a dark-blue drapery, save for one bare arm held aloft, a hip, and both legs. The puddle of drapery at the figure's feet helps to ground her even as she is silhouetted against a vivid flame-red field that bears a repetitive leaf pattern stenciled in gold. A serpentine garland of stylized green leaves begins to encircle her body, a motif that is continued on the two side panels where they describe ogee curves that rise up the length of the screen. The background is again flame-red. On the left-hand panel, in gold thread, is embroidered in a Fraktur font "She'd always been the apple," and on the right panel, "Of Adam's eye." On the reverse of the central panel the text continues, "Temptation my ass, desire has its place, and besides, they were both doomed from the start."

This screen helps establish the reading of the larger installation. By invoking characteristics of the Old Testament story of Genesis, Weems places us at the beginning, in the Garden of Eden. As Museum of Modern Art curator Thomas W. Collins, Jr., points out, "In [the] retelling of this creation myth...[Weems] highlight[s] [her] own particular understanding of the gender difference and the dynamics of heterosexual relationships that necessarily arise from this difference."[26] With this series, Weems asks us to challenge the tradition upon which these relationships are based, the male-female divide, constructed in opposition in our very mythology, in this case, the Bible. As Weems herself, tells us, "The image and text on the screen challenge a number of assumptions about sexual desire, about religious belief, and about looking.... The installation is in some ways about how men and women are accomplices in their own downfall, in their own oppression, in their own victimization."[27] For as the re-created story of Adam and Eve ends, they have been expelled from Eden and have claimed opposite sides of a wide valley, she with her dominion over cupboard, bedroom, and cradle; he with his throne from which to wield the tools of power.

In 1994, Weems was invited by the J. Paul Getty Museum to prepare a body of work that reacted to a historical exhibition the museum was mounting entitled "Hidden Witness: African Americans in Early Photography." These daguerreotypes, tintypes, and ambrotypes of African Americans, dating from the 1840s through the 1860s, a time span that includes both years of slavery and emancipation, were drawn from the Getty's holdings and the private collection of Jackie Napolean Wilson, a black attorney from Detroit. The images included family groups, women with children, musicians, soldiers, formal portraits of individuals, abolitionists, freemen, as well as scenes that record historic occasions. The show took its title from an 1855 daguerreotype depicting a white family posed in front of their Greek Revival home. In the background is a black male servant holding a shovel, engaged in yardwork.

In response to this show, Weems appropriated some of these nineteenth-century photographs of blacks as well as twentieth-century photographs of African Americans taken from popular media and by other photographers, including Robert Frank and Robert Mapplethorpe. She rephotographed the images, enlarged them, monoprinted them in a febrile red, and mounted them in a circle-cut black mat. The glass that covers each framed piece has been sandblasted with text that either categorizes the individual to whose portrait it is appended, or creates a brief narrative statement that can be read alone or as part of the larger narrative that emerges when the thirty-two photoworks are taken as a whole.

Entitled *From Here I Saw What Happened and I Cried,* the series takes us to life after Eden and shows us the results of the power struggle waged previously in the garden. When we left them, Eve was destined to control hearth and home; Adam had the throne and temporal rule. "Banished from the heavenly garden of earthly delight they landed head first smack in the middle of a tradition that denied them both." Their destinies foretold, we now see Eve, head wrapped and expression leveled, caught behind the caption "You became Mammie, Mama, Mother & then, Yes, Confidant—Ha." Adam is old and white bearded: "Descending the Throne You became Foot Soldier & Cook."

The series is introduced by a photograph of a West African tribeswoman, a sort of anthropological shot of her in profile, bare to the waist and with an elaborate coiffure. She is toned blue (as in "singing the blues"), and her caption reads, "From Here I Saw What Happened." At the end of the series her mirror image appears, again toned blue; her caption concludes, "And I Cried." The visual character of the introductory and concluding images in this series contain elements of parody. They can be viewed as sentimentalized visions of African natives, bare to the waist, ethnographic portraits, timeless yet frozen in time. Does this woman represent the Africans who were left behind, unchanged over these hundreds of years? Her pitying, pitiful, and impotent response to the diaspora implicates us: our own view is just as steeped in time, observed at a similar safe remove. She places the real action and evolution of the story on our own shores and connects us by this dispassionate observation.

From Here I Saw What Happened and I Cried is, itself, composed of images from the past—some are nineteenth-century, but even those from the twentieth century are distanced from the present. The images don't really date past the Civil Rights movement, except for Weems's appropriation of Robert Mapplethorpe's *Man in Polyester Suit,* and its subject of desire defies time. What is Weems telling us about our moment of history? What is our relationship to past injustices? Have any lessons been learned from history, or are we doomed to repeat inequities? Weems would like us to think about how a social system involving slavery came into being, how it was allowed to flourish, what cultural, philosophical, and economic structures gave it life. Slavery was an economic system that relied on the controlling of human resources—how does that continue to play out; does it? Did the desires, needs, and pursuits of the culture that envisioned and implemented slavery change or disappear, or do they continue to be met? How? The answers are not here, but the questions are persuasive.

It is clear by now that Carrie Mae Weems is a question asker. Her goal is not to offer us answers but to put us in an environment where many questions can be posed. *Who What When Where* is the title of one of her most recent installations. The title, of course, is composed of four interrogatory words, which pose the four questions we seek to answer in constructing any story. This installation addresses the questions of class and social systems but offers no single or clear reading. It also explores Weems's relationship to art history, part of an ongoing investigation that has so far touched on artists Robert Colescott, Frida Kahlo, and Willem de Kooning, among others. With this series, she turns her eye on the Russian Constructivists, the artistic arm of the Russian Revolution of 1917, and asks us to consider whether artistic social engagement can influence individual and social development. In this theatrical assemblage of digitally reproduced photographs, banners, neon signs, and large-scale free-standing sculptures, we are placed in a terrain of unexpected associations.

There are three especially striking and strikingly dissimilar components to *Who What When Where*. Among these is a ten-foot-high by twelve-foot-long digitally reproduced appropriated photograph on canvas of graduation day at the United States Military Academy at West Point. It's a very active composition: young cadets in dress-whites caught in a wide range of dynamic body positions, arms angled, heads thrown back, mouths open as they watch their white hats sail through the air. It is a scene of general exultation, one might even say of *jouissance*. Along the length of the top of the canvas, a caption has been dropped out in white block letters: HIP-HIP HOORAY, ONCE AGAIN CAPITALISM IS SAVED. Here we have a reconfigured documentary photograph, digitally reproduced. From a distance, its surface appears to be as seamless as that of a gelatin-silver print. As we get closer, the digital image is revealed to be composed of many dots, the surface seems to be breaking down. By metaphorical extension, we might consider the political order represented as destabilized.

A six-foot-high steel reconstruction of Vladimir Tatlin's *Monument to the Third International* is placed directly in front of the large-scale photomural. The never-realized monument, known as Tatlin's Tower, was commissioned and designed in 1919 as a physical embodiment of the socially progressive goals of artists during the early days of the Russian Revolution. The tower is a dynamic, open-worked structure composed of two intertwined spirals braced by a massive sloping strut. The monument seems to lean energetically forward, even as its spiral thread appears to screw up out of the ground and into the air. Meant to rise three times as high as the Eiffel Tower, Tatlin's Tower was to have housed the executive, administrative, and propaganda offices of the new Communist order.[28]

It is possible to consider Tatlin's Tower anthropomorphically, for its abstract form has a metaphorical resemblance to the human figure. There is its characteristic lean, which can be seen as a stride forward; the massive sloping strut can be viewed as a spine; and the intertwined spirals as forming a rib cage around the meeting halls—the structure's organs. Schematic representations of the latter, the meeting halls, always figure in Tatlin's drawings and maquettes for the tower, but are left out of Weems's model. It's as if she were showing the tower eviscerated, a skeletal husk.

Weems likes to point out that Tatlin's design for the monument was influenced by ancient Muslim architecture, especially the minaret of the Great Mosque of al-Mutawakkil at Samarra in Iraq.[29] This neatly relates the tower to the mosques Weems photographed in Djenné and included in the *Africa Series*. It underscores our reading of Tatlin's Tower as a male space. In Weems's installation, the complex forms contained in Tatlin's Tower are sited so that they mirror the thrusts and angles of the male bodies in the photomural it accompanies. Rising up in priapic glory, the tower extends the notion of *jouissance* that the photograph suggests.

The final element of the installation that I wish to consider are four large digitally reproduced photographic still lifes of everyday objects—a typewriter, a book, a clock, and a globe of the world. Each sepia-toned image bears a one-word inscription printed along its bottom edge: the typewriter has *Who,* the book *What,* the clock *When,* and the globe *Where.* As in so many of Weems's photo series and installations, it is the combination of image and text that helps to suggest a reading of the larger installation. Here the narrative waits to be constructed as we answer some questions: *Who* is the author or the authority, whose is the voice that gets heard, recorded, written down? *What* is our system of knowledge, what do we believe, what are our rules and philosophies? *When* asks us to consider the temporal, history, evolution, continuity, and the now. *Where* directs us to think globally, to question the notion of mapping, and draws us to a specific site—the shorelines of the Atlantic.

It is useful to remember that these very four still lifes were among the fifteen large-format Polaroid photographs in Weems's 1991 installation *And 22 Million Very Tired and Very Angry People*. There she mixed photographs with captions and banners bearing texts selected from the writings of revolutionaries and social activists, including Malcolm X, Stuart Hall, and Rosa Luxemburg. *And 22 Million...*, which immediately preceded the *Sea Islands Series*, was seen as creating "an emotional universe inhabited by individuals committed to ending domination, oppression, and injustice around the world."[30] Reviewing the captions that accompanied these four images in the 1991 installation enhances our understanding of them now: The typewriter was described as "An Informational System"; the book, "Some Theory"; the clock, "A Precise Moment in Time"; and the globe, "A Hot Spot in a Corrupt World."

In considering the efficacy of artistic social commitment in the face of triumphant world capitalism, Weems is questioning her own quest, wondering if her social engagement has been in vain. Her initial goal of using images to deconstruct the essentialism of black representation, to expose the interconnections of race and class, of gender and sexism, has begun to be seen as impossible to convey to a broad audience: "I started with lofty ideas about social change," she now says. "I believed one could change the world. I've grown to question how that is possible. Dealing with future possibilities is much more complicated when dealing with now."

Even so, Carrie Mae Weems does fundamentally believe in the possibility for social change. "I'm a sucker for hope!" she exclaims.[31] Each act of resistance, intervention, and contestation builds on the ones that occurred before. "By doing something systematically," she contends, "we don't know what's possible, we only know our historical moment." John Berger tackles this conundrum in his book *Art & Revolution:* "There is always a danger that the relative freedom of art can render it meaningless. Yet it is this same freedom which allows art, and art alone, to express and preserve the profoundest expectations of a period. It is part of the nature of man to expect more than he can immediately achieve. His expectations are never independent of necessity, but *the necessary should never be confused with the immediate.*"[32]

That sense of potentiality and the mounting history of social resistance is at the center of Weems's most recent installation, *Ritual & Revolution*. It is a beautiful, delicate work, similar to some things that have come before it, but more direct in addressing our senses and emotions. With this piece, Weems creates a tactile, translucent, acoustic environment composed of digitally reproduced photographs printed on ten to twelve freely hanging muslin banners, suspended from a gallery ceiling. They are hung in a pyramid formation with enough space to walk among them.

Ritual & Revolution references and borrows installation strategies, imagery, and text that have appeared before in other works. The use of banners was a primary feature in the installation of *And 22 Million Very Tired and Very Angry People,* where, imprinted with agitational texts, they were reminders of the traditional political and public functions banners have served. In *Ritual & Revolution* the banners are printed with photographs of ancient ruins, statuary, and landscapes. Some of the images we see on the banners have been recycled—we recognize a Djenné street scene, for instance. But the others—a pair of images of Assyrian temple steps; a pair of korai, Greek maidens, holding hares; a Japanese rock garden; a ruined courtyard in the city of Tulum, Mexico; a park with an allée of trees; and a rugged seascape—expand the geographical, historical, and cultural range of consideration.

Rather than written text, this work relies on the artist's own voice reciting an ode-like expository that fills the gallery space with warmly solemn tones. Here Weems revisits a technique she employed in *Family Pictures and Stories,* where she recited family narratives on audiotape that could be accessed by headphones. Now the sound of her voice recounting a world history takes a more insistent role in the creation of an enveloping acoustical environment.

"Between the two worlds/I was with you/but as the wind on the Caspian Sea." So begins the narrative. The position of the voice is hard to specify and is not of one individual. The ephemeral voice alternates between an all-observing narrator who sees the unfolding of our interior lives—our struggles for identity, our fears, our failings, our greed, our deaths—and an experienced participant who encompasses history and who was with us during epochal struggles—the Middle Passage, the Storming of the Bastille, the October Revolution, the Potato Famine, Nazi Germany. As we have seen before, this double voice recalls the tradition of signifying exemplified by the writings of Zora Neale Hurston. Something Henry Louis Gates tells us about Hurston seems especially pertinent here: "The narrative voice Hurston created is a lyrical and disembodied yet individual voice, from which emerges a singular longing and utterance, a transcendent...self, extending far beyond the merely individual."[33]

In *Ritual & Revolution,* Weems pictures herself at the center of the installation, a self-portrait of the artist as everywoman, dressed in timeless draperies, eyes closed, head tilted as she listens, along with us, to the recitation that unfolds around us. She is in the work and outside of it, assuming the role of participant and external narrator. This sublimation of the individual in the communal is at the heart of Weems's continual quest for an art practice that engages the viewer in a joined effort to challenge received knowledge, construct new readings out of decentered truths, and effect change. As the recitation ends, Weems closes on an expectant note: "In the twilight/coming on a day without end/Anna traced the tracks of your tears/& I could see again/the coming of Spring's hope/in the May flowers/of May Days/long forgotten."

NOTES

1. "Carrie Mae Weems, Artist," *Alpert Awards, Visual Arts, 1996,* 1996 (HYPERLINK http://www.alpertawards.com/archive/Weems.html, 17 June 1998).
2. Carrie Mae Weems, interview with Thomas W. Collins, Jr., *Projects 52* (New York: Museum of Modern Art, 1995), np.
3. Carrie Mae Weems, as quoted in *Aperture,* 129 (Fall 1992), 47.
4. This and all subsequent quotations attributed to Carrie Mae Weems are taken from a series of interviews conducted between the author and Weems during 1997 and 1998, unless otherwise stated.
5. The term "black Atlantic" alludes to the syncretic culture, originating from contact between the Old World and the New, that connects black persons of western Africa and the western hemisphere. See Robert Farris Thompson, *Flash of the Spirit, African and Afro-American Art and Philosophy* (New York: Vintage Books, 1984) and Paul Gilroy, *The Black Atlantic, Modernity and Double Consciousness* (Cambridge, MA: Harvard University Press, 1993).
6. Carrie Mae Weems, interview with bell hooks, "Talking Art with Carrie Mae Weems," in *Art on My Mind* (New York: The New Press, 1995), 76.
7. bell hooks, "Diasporic Landscapes of Longing," in *Carrie Mae Weems* (Philadelphia: The Fabric Workshop/Museum, 1994), 31.
8. Mel Rosenthal, "Commentary," in *Nueva Luz 2* (New York: En Foco, 1989), 32.
9. bell hooks, "Talking Art with Carrie Mae Weems," op. cit., 91.
10. Michele Wallace, "'Why Are There No Great Black Artists?' The Problem of Visuality in African-American Culture," in *Black Popular Culture,* ed. Gina Dent (Seattle: Bay Press, 1992), 333–46.
11. Craig Watters, "Images of Black America," Ph.D. diss. proposal, Syracuse University, 1998.
12. bell hooks, "Diasporic Landscapes of Longing," op. cit., 31–32.
13. Henry Louis Gates, Jr., *The Signifying Monkey* (New York: Oxford University Press, 1988), xxiv.
14. Andreas Hapkemeyer and Peter Weiermair, eds., *photo text text photo* (Kilchberg/Zurich, Switzerland: Edition Stemmle AG, 1996), 10–11.
15. Henry Louis Gates, Jr., op. cit.
16. W. E. Burghaardt Du Bois, *The Souls of Black Folk* (1903; reprint, New York: Dodd, Mead & Company, 1961), 3.
17. Zora Neale Hurston (1903–1960), an important figure in the Harlem Renaissance, was a novelist, folklorist, and anthropologist, who pioneered a storytelling style that fused each element of her training.
18. Carrie Mae Weems, interview with Leslie King-Hammond, in *Who What When Where* (New York: The Whitney Museum of American Art, 1998), np.
19. Henry Louis Gates, Jr., op. cit., 183.
20. Ibid., 181.
21. Margaret Washington Creel, "Gullah Attitudes toward Life and Death," in *Africanisms in American Culture,* ed. Joseph E. Holloway (Bloomington and Indianapolis: Indiana University Press, 1990), 70.
22. Henry Louis Gates, Jr., op. cit., 4.
23. John Edward Phillips, "The African Heritage of White America," in *Africanisms in American Culture,* op. cit., 225–39.
24. Carrie Mae Weems, interview with Thomas W. Collins, Jr., op. cit., np.
25. Robert Farris Thompson enhances our understanding of mosque architecture as male space:

"When [the architectural historian Labelle] Proussin asked the master mason of Djenné, M. Be Sao, to give reasons for the beauty of the Friday Mosque, he answered, 'Because [the clay pillars] are tall and straight like a man.'" In Robert Farris Thompson, *Face of the Gods: Art and Altars of Africa and the African Americas* (New York: The Museum for African Art, 1993), 118.

26. Thomas W. Collins, Jr., op. cit., np.
27. Carrie Mae Weems, interview with Thomas W. Collins, Jr., op. cit., np.
28. John Milner, "The Monument to the Third International," in *Vladimir Tatlin and the Russian Avant-Garde* (New Haven and London: Yale University Press, 1983), 151–80.
29. John Milner suggests that it is possible that Tatlin had visited the Great Mosque of Samarra as a young seaman, in John Milner, op. cit., 243, note 7.
30. bell hooks, "Diasporic Landscapes of Longing," op. cit., 70.
31. Carrie Mae Weems, interview with Thomas W. Collins, Jr., op. cit., np.
32. John Berger, *Art & Revolution* (1969; reprint, New York: Vintage International, 1997), 47.
33. Henry Louis Gates, Jr., op. cit., 183.

SOME THOUGHTS ON CARRIE MAE WEEMS

When I first saw Carrie Mae Weems's *Kitchen Table* (1990), I immediately confused her with her creation, the character featured in the photographs. I confused her position as subject and her role as author. I assumed the details of the text of the piece to be completely autobiographical. It was a common, although grave, mistake. The problem of untangling Weems as subject and Weems as author persists as I continue to engage with her work.

This early encounter with *Kitchen Table* and my fascination with its visual and textual narrative remained with me as I worked on what would be an exhibition I organized in 1994 entitled "Black Male: Representations of Masculinity in Contemporary American Art." As I gave thought to shaping the exhibition, I remembered *Kitchen Table* and the way it struck me as being intensely about black masculinity. The narrative, while powered by a female voice and view, takes a deep and probing look at a relationship between a black man and a black woman. In the narrator's voice we hear love and romance colliding with desire, resentment, need, and acceptance. It was a rare narrative and encouraged me to think more deeply about the idea of exploring the construction of the black male image through a multitude of viewpoints, not all black and not all male. It was an obvious methodology but only became clear through my engagement with this and Weems's other works.

FROM HERE...

At about the time "Black Male" was presented in Los Angeles, Weems's project *From Here I Saw What Happened and I Cried* (1995) was on view at the J. Paul Getty Museum. Considered by some to be Weems's most significant work to date and discussed by many as one of the most important artworks of the decade, the project, then and now, provides an interesting place from which to consider her work in general. It was commissioned as a response to an exhibition at the Getty of rare photographs of African Americans from the 1840s to the 1860s entitled "Hidden Witness: African Americans in Early Photography." One of its purposes seems to have been to provoke a contemporary reading of this historic, problematic group of images. What Weems did was perhaps even more subversive than the institutionally sanctioned subversion inherent in the act of commissioning her. Her phototext installation created an alternative history that simultaneously embraced and rejected what the museum's photographs represented. Instead of simply exhibiting one of her own extant pieces, she courageously and critically read the museum's show through her own new series of works. She expressed that reading in her texts, which accompanied her photographs. In the vernacular, to read is to critique, to create a metadiscourse around an idea. It is to think and respond actively and acutely with wit and irony. Weems's piece is an incredible read. It critiques the entire history of black visual representation. It is not a simplistic genealogy; rather, it encompasses and acknowledges her collusion with and desire for this rich visual history.

From Here... begins with an archival photograph of an African woman. The text and colored, rephotographed images create a chronology that takes us from that African woman through the documents that picture African Americans as they were and as they were imagined by others—as they pictured themselves and as they were pictured. The text is like a tone poem as it relates, in the first person, the story behind the graphic photographs. The piece ends up where it began, with the African woman, appearing with the text "and I cried," a plaintive rejoinder to the beginning of the project's title. This ending choice is curious, because while critics wrote about how the piece was resolved, its ending to me seems unresolved. This lack of neat resolution is the project's subtext. Unlike nearly all of Weems's other work, it leaves questions unanswered and the viewer in a place similar to that of the narrator. What made this project unconventional, what made it so important and timely, was not just its site (though the overwhelming Eurocentric emphasis of the Getty collection and its program made it ripe for a contemporary intervention), but the more nuanced combination of the original exhibition, the artist and her project, and the history they shared in the process of black image making.

From Here... begs the question, from where? Weems's career has been well documented, and the lineage between her works and the attendant themes they address provides a place from which the concerns of the work developed. *From Here...* underscores the sited nature of her work, her ability to respond, her desire to analyze from fifteen or twenty different perspectives: exhibiting at the Getty, in Los Angeles after the Rodney King riots, within the context of black history and black art history, to name just a few. Where did this work come from? Influence is a tricky question when considering Carrie Mae Weems's work because her practice is so marked by originality. In many ways her early work was an indirect antecedent of the photographs featured in "Hidden Witness." Her early documentary work inspired by the Black Photographers Annual and other related black photographic collectives sought to picture African-American culture in an unbiased, unadulterated way. In her earliest works, pictures of her family, Weems delved head-on into the slippery territory of positive and negative images, making clear the passion and dexterity necessary to avoid the facile aspects of this paradigm. *From Here...* was not simply a response but a corrective gesture. It provided the basis to understand the discourse about black visual representation in America from the nascent period "Hidden Witness" addresses to the present.

From Here... positions Weems on an interesting axis that, depending on one's vantage point, places her at the auspicious beginning of one moment or as the final word at the end of another. These poles, to define them one way, would be the historic past of the Black Arts Movement and the yet to be named black aesthetic present. Another place to site her would be between the dissonant trajectories of feminism and multiculturalism. Yet another axis would be that between traditional photography and contemporary, conceptually based photography. Weems's project weaves through various extremities, synthesizing the various aspects within her work. It is a remarkable and affecting ability.

Having just crafted an exhibition on the problematic of representation, I realized that, with *From Here...,* Weems had rendered my plodding methodology somewhat obsolete. Most who attempt to examine representation, particularly black representation, will undoubtedly find the task overwhelming. I approached her project as a curator who is not an artist but came to terms with her incredible engagement as she, an artist, temporarily moved into the curatorial arena with this piece. She worked from a place that was not just personal, but that, without being didactic, conveyed a sense of the curatorial responsibility to teach. I also began to think of her project in relation to others that had affected the cultural zeitgeist in an equally powerful way. I found precedents in both Fred Wilson's project for the Baltimore Historical Society titled *Mining the Museum* and Joseph Kosuth's project for the Brooklyn Museum called *The Play of the Unmentionables.* Both of these projects redefined the role of the visual artist in relation to the museum. They deftly reversed the balance of power between the artist and the institution.

Most significantly, I came to this work thinking of Weems in the many roles she simultaneously occupied: artist, reader, writer, and thinker. I left profoundly focused on her voice. As in my earlier mistaken recognition of her as the subject and author of her work, I once again experienced the vertiginous effect of acknowledging the voice of her art and the art of her voice.

Once I heard Weems read from Toni Morrison's novel *Jazz.* The occasion was a panel discussion with two other artists. Instead of speaking about her own work, Weems read a passage from the very beginning of Morrison's novel that, even on the page, conjured rich visual imagery. She approached the words as a singer would a sound, creating an image somewhere between Morrison's intention and her own interpretation. Her reading made her own work more understandable. It made it clear that her words were less about text and more about voice. They were meant to be read and the sound of the words and their cadences heard. After that experience, I would listen to Weems many times and revisit her work to try again and again to hear her.

I SAW WHAT HAPPENED...

In conversation, Weems has an amazing capacity for description. She can recall the shape and size and feel of things and convey them to her listener. She will recount a story or an experience with vivid detail. She gives even a simple detail incredible texture with her choice of words and acute observations. A short while ago I took a trip to place I had never been. Weems was also there. On this trip we were in the same place, at the same time, doing almost the same things. Still, I was completely compelled by Weems's description of the places, people, and events. It is not that I didn't trust or value my own impressions, but that hers made me reconsider what I was seeing and what I was experiencing. The richness of a conversation with her carries over into her work.

Weems's work is an inspired partnership of vision and voice. In a way, each body of her work poses a question and then, through the work, image and text, answers it. This process and its attendant product align her with many of the artists of her generation who see their relationship to their audience as an active, ongoing dialogue. In her two series the *Sea Islands Series* (1991–92) and the *Africa Series* (1993) the questions asked are intriguingly fettered. The *Sea Islands Series* has her looking for Africa, asking where it resonates in African-American culture. This issue of Africa is a loaded one because it comes attached to a large, fractious debate about the role of Africa in contemporary America. In this group of photographs she captures what is left of the mythic history of Africa, reaching back to her training as a folklorist to document the mores and customs of a culture slipping away from this notion into a newly defined America. In the images that feature the splendor and beauty of the region, she both pictures the existing realities of the land and lets you imagine what is not there, what might have been. In her accompanying texts, she shatters any sense of romanticism that the images might conjure. She finds "Uncombed heads/acrylic nails &/Afrocentric attitudes that Africans find laughable." Ultimately she finds and photographs a truth unable to support a long-held fiction of an idyllic paradise. This work is often spoken about in relation to Julie Dash's film *Daughters of the Dust,* which also documents this culture. Dash, however, reconstructs the past, while Weems, taking the harder job, reckons with the present. In what must be a precedent to her images in the Getty project, this series begins with three-toned, appropriated photographs of captured members of the Gullah tribe. Created originally as documentation, they provide the tonic note for this piece. They are the crucial link both to her understanding of the uses of photography and her need for the images that both she and others create. This is a difficult work, made more so by its unflinching beauty. It is difficult for what is in its texts and images and what is left unspoken and unseen.

The *Africa Series* seems to pose the question that was asked by the *Sea Islands Series,* except in an intriguing turn, it creates a fiction out of the truths she encounters rather than finds a truth deep within the fictions. Rather than looking for Africa, she goes to Africa. There, she encounters the gender-specific architectural tradition and the structures that are the architectural artifacts of the slave trade, which she documents with beautiful, richly toned prints. She imagines the creation myth, placing Eve at the center of a sensuous tale. This work also sees Weems moving fully into three-dimensional installation, begun by the inclusion of discrete objects in the *Sea Islands Series*. The photographs were exhibited with real African artifacts: traditional ladders and a bed. The central feature of the installation was a screen on which Weems appears seductively shrouded. The installation is knitted together with wallpaper created from an image of a black woman appropriated from the endsheets of a George Bernard Shaw book. Her topics here are Africa, slavery, architecture, cultural artifacts, black female agency and sexuality, religion, and mythology. Expansive, seemingly unrelated, and dense, this work brings her practice to a stirring, culminating apex. This looking and finding and creating is what places her squarely within the context of contemporary art practice. The core of her work is conceptual, girded by her investment in the documentary tradition and her interdisciplinary approach to her practice, which subsumes history, literature, and music into her project.

Belying the myth that conceptual artists disdain the old-fashioned notion of aesthetics, Weems has long been consumed and galvanized by the idea of beauty. The notion of beauty encompasses and reaches beyond aesthetics. It is not a simple concept, as often there are unspoken political implications in her use. She'll say, "she's a beautiful sister," which is not simply about being pretty, or talk about a feeling being beautiful, which is not simply being happy. Beauty is a powerful adjective in her hands and an important tool in her work. Her work is always about beauty and purposely so. She seduces the viewer through the very process of creating luscious prints, or beautiful images, without ever using beauty purely to seduce. Beauty is always tempered by other concerns that take the viewer beyond aesthetics. But no matter what one encounters within the text or within one's own revelations about what the texts ultimately say, the religion of beauty always undergirds Weems's vision and informs her work.

AND I CRIED.

The subject of a recent conference was the use of stereotypical images of African Americans in contemporary American art, a topic at the edge of current debate. No matter that this was not a new area of inquiry for black or white artists. For every unquestionably stereotypical image in the annals of American art by a white artist, there was an image created of African Americans by an African American that was equally reviled. Despite the open environment created by postmodernism and multiculturalism, the idea of essentially negative and positive images was openly debated. The core of the debate centered around two distinct groups of African-American artists, demarcated more by ideology than by generation. The debate ranged far and wide, many aspersions were cast, and little, if anything, was resolved. An immutable tension hung in the air as personal and aesthetic ideals were intermingled. At a moment close to the proposed end of the gathering, Weems got up to speak. Although, given the nature and trajectory of her work, she could have moved to either side of the debate, she graciously thanked and acknowledged those artists in the room whose work helped define the discourse. She placed herself within the context of those artists who demanded the need to express a spectrum of points of view. She opened up the points of confluence and attempted to chart a genealogy that put the debate, while urgent and necessary, in its appropriate context. She sanctioned the freedoms of all artists while stressing the need for all to acknowledge artistic debts and legacies. In this way, she reached out and closed the enormous gulf between the divided participants.

From Here I Saw What Happened and I Cried conveys a sentiment encompassed in her entire body of work. It is a statement that has connections to each body that preceded it and each that has followed. At present, Weems is charting another course. Using the form of the three-dimensional installation, she has moved her focus into more far-reaching examinations involving more broadly based political ideals. Here, class enters her work as a dominant concern. More globally translatable than race, more pliant than gender, and more trenchant than sexuality, class brings her work into a new arena. This trajectory seems natural; Weems has evolved aesthetically from the self to the community to the world, each time casting her net further. This moment also figures Weems as an artist committed to using and understanding emotion as effectively and as precisely as intellect.

Her meditation on the images she assembled for the Getty project ends "and I cried." It is a personal conceit, perhaps the most personal ever to appear in her work. It casts her presence fully into her practice and from her practice into our lives. Weems is the most accessible contemporary artist. Her work is about reverent enjoyment, not just for her audience, but for herself.

————————————————————————————————SEA ISLANDS SERIES

1991-92

Lots of slaves brought over from Africa could fly. There folks can fly even now. They tell me them people could do all kinda curious things. They could even make farm tools work for em just by talkin to em. And some of em could disappear at will. Wist! And they'd be gone!!

Ole man Waldburg own slaves, and worked them hard and one day they was hoein' in the field and the driver come over and two of em was up under the shade tree and the hoe was working by itself. The driver say, "What's this?" and they say,

Kum Buba Yali
Jum Bumba Tambe,
Kum Kunka Yali, Kum Kuma Tambe

Quick like. Then they rize off the ground and flew back to Africa. Nobody ever see em no more. My grandmother see that with her own eyes. Anytime they wanted they would fly back to Africa, then come back again to the plantation. They'd come back cause they have chillun who didn't have the power to fly and had to stay on the plantation.

Plate 2

Plate 3

Plate 4

EBO LANDING

One midnight at high tide a ship bringing a cargo of Ebo (Ibo) men landed at Dunbar Creek on the Island of St. Simons. But the men refused to be sold into slavery; joining hands together they turned back toward the water, chanting, "the water brought us, the water will take us away." They all drowned, but to this day when the breeze sighs over the marshes and through the trees, you can hear the clank of chains and echo of their chant at Ebo Landing.

Plate 5

Plate 6

THE
HOUSE

When you move into
a new house, remove old
spirits by washing around the windows and doors with vinegar water. But,
prevent spirits from crossing the doorstep by
putting salt and pepper along the door and window sills.

Trimming the windows in blue will ward off hags,
witches and other evil spirits.

Wall paper your home with newspaper. Before a hag can bother
you, it must read every word. And if it can't read, then there you go.
But newspaper strung between an antenna will do the job too.

Place rice in the four corners of your home for good luck and
put a glass of water in a corner to absorb evil spirits.

A kitchen knife stuck into the wood over the door will keep
witches out of the house when the family is away.

If you swept dust out of the house at sunset you just might sweep away
the spirit of a family member.

Never build an addition to your house. A home can never be extended.

BONEYARD

    alarm clocks wake the dead on judgment day
    kerosene lamps light the path to glory
    the last cup, plate and spoon used by the departed
    should be placed on the grave
    keep a child safe from a dead person's spirit
    by passing the child over the dead person's
    body or coffin

If you suspect that a person has been killed by hoodoo, put a cassava stick in the hand and he will punish the murderer. If he was killed by violence, put the stick in one hand and a knife and fork in the other. The spirit of the murdered one will first drive the slayer insane, and then kill him with great violence.

If people die wishing to see someone, they will stay limp and warm for days. They are still waiting.

If a person dies who has not had his fling in this world, he will turn on his face in his grave.

    I got a black cat bone
    I got a mojo tooth
    I got John the Conqueroo
    I'm gonna mess with you

Plate 7

Plate 8

Plate 9

Plate 10

Plates 12

AFRICA SERIES

1993

Knowing that the power of generations coursed through her alone, she was saddened by their great contest in which there were no winners. So it came to pass that, yes, she held the keys to the kingdom but took no joy in the power of her subterfuge.

Plate 14

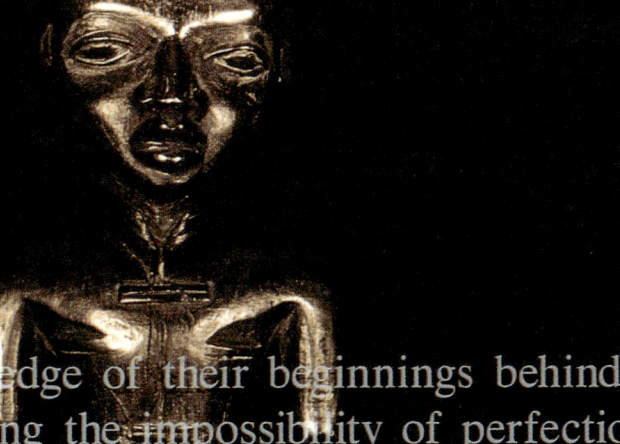

With the knowledge of their beginnings behind him, and recognizing the impossibility of perfection in this life, yes he ruled with the tools of power from his throne, but focused his desire for unity of oneness with woman in the hereafter.

Plate 15

Plate 16

When Allah put Adam and Eve in the Garden, he lowered bread and grapes to them, so that they would have something to eat. Adam and Eve were still alone at that time, had not yet met, and had not had sexual relations. Ha. They'd both been looking high and low. Unveiled, save for her pendéli, he saw her first resting in the shade of the bombax tree. It was thus that he spied the first meaning of Samson and Delilah, the lion's den, and all that was to come, thinking to himself: this is definitely my kinda woman.

He said, I have been looking for you each day; have you been looking for me? Excited by his presence, but feeling coy, determined not to reveal her hand, she told the first lie: I've remained always in one place and have not moved from it. Wanting an equal, she wanted to be impressed; she knew she was impressive. Besides, her virginity certificate was written in black ink.

So he came strumming the cora, bearing gifts of cowrie shells and cola nuts, blowing star-dust memories, dazzling her senses by recounting his powers:

> I can build a castle from a single grain of sand
> I can make a ship sail on dry land
> I can change a river into a raging fire
> I can live forever if my soul desires

Heaven lies at the feet of women

Her mouth like cherry wine, liquid and set, her rich body round, soft and supple; her breasts large playful at the tip; her secret garden wild as musk. A maddening jungle, joyous to behold. Oh my!! When he touched her, she smiled, merrily, laughing pearls of effervescence and he knew her love would be boundless. Landing he felt gold-dust, sapphires, daffodils in the halo surrounding her being. Climbing up his legs, crossing the expanse of his Mandingo chest, dangling briefly from the hairs of his arms, she perched her loveliness upon a shoulder blade, blowing Mood Indigo gently in his ear. Together they knew something more. Ha!! They knew no doubles, felt no shame and walked the thin line of pain and pleasure. Enlightenment became their friend. Ha. And they both moaned.

He said, Heaven must be like this. And she said, silly-boy I am Heaven. Ha. And the mule of the world too. Ha. I do hope you know what to do with me, for through me is the knowing and meaning of ourselves. HA! She was modest, but facts were facts.

S(he) was as tempting as temptation. And in this way time passed mingled with fragrant Arabian nights.

Sébéréssé, all things have their hour

Plate 17

Plate 18

Plate 19

Wrapped as they were in their magic, dripping from honey poured from the calabash, they needed more than love to stave off the hunger nipping at their bud. Neither with certainty remembered suggesting eating from the tree in the garden, but somehow or another the decision had been made. It could have been her; she was a curious rebellious woman for sure. On the other hand, he was a man enraptured with the spices of life. One thing was certain, this was the ending and the beginning of things. Square-toed and flat-footed they danced before the lawd with all their might, but evidently it was too late. Banished from the heavenly garden of earthly delight they landed head first smack in the middle of a tradition that denied them both. Even the lion, sovereign beast of the savanna kingdom, cried for them.

A woman is like an apricot,
eighteen days and she is out season

Against this back drop, ha, and in the eyes of the almighty, ha, he denounced her; claiming for himself alone the tools of power. Shocked by his betrayal, but no fool, she turned to the ruler of darkness, acquiring three keys.

        one to the cupboard
        one to the bedroom
        one to the cradle

She fought him like a champ, but neither won, it was much more complicated than that. With his tools of power and her keys to the kingdom they stood face to face on top of their own mountain with a swing-low valley between them.

        A man is like the hands of a clock,
        he points in all directions

Plate 21

Made for him, she represented the perfect woman.

Plate 22

Made for her, he represented the perfect man.

She'd always been the apple

FROM HERE I SAW WHAT HAPPENED AND I CRIED
1995-96

Plate 24

Plate 25

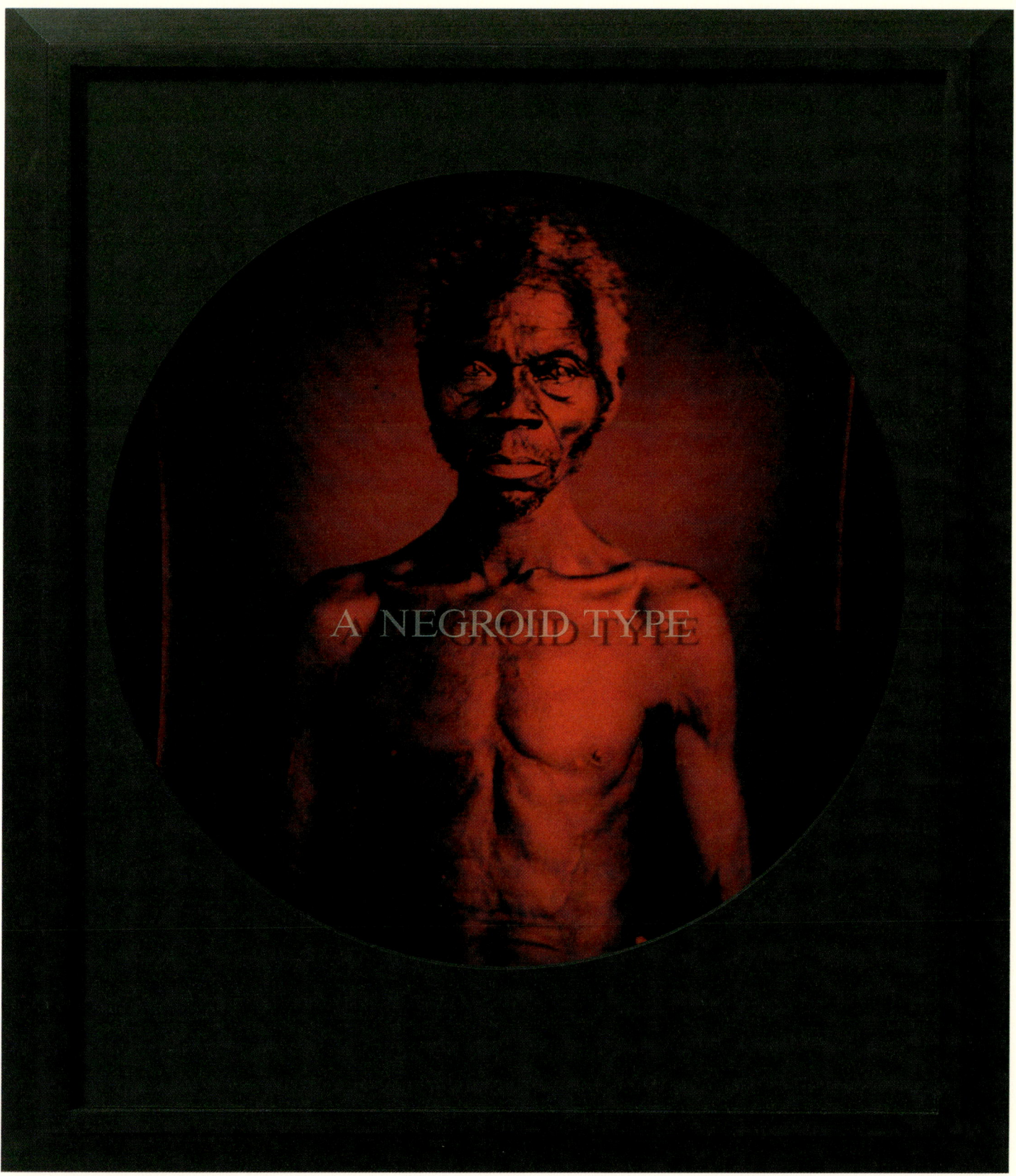

Plate 26

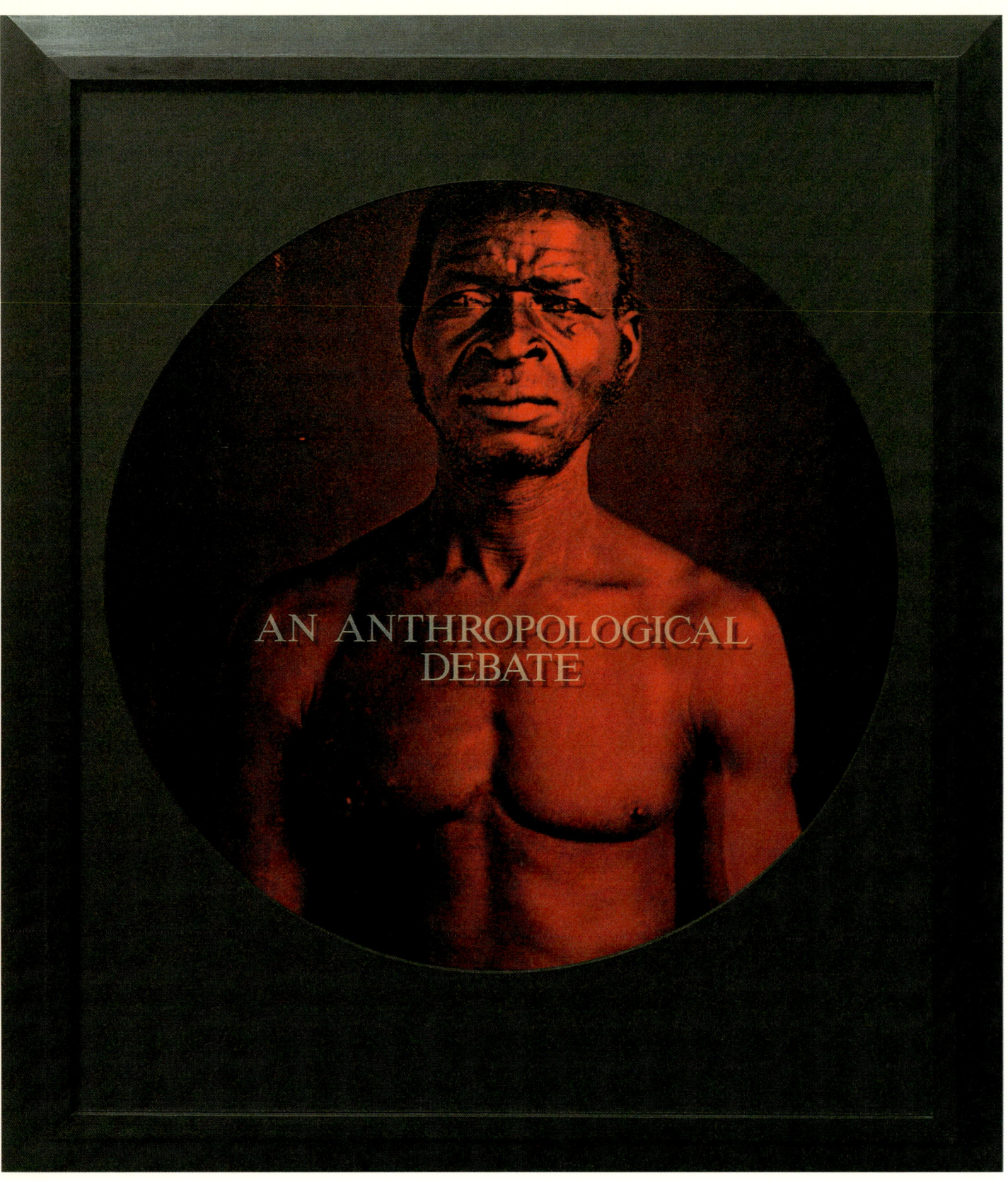

Plate 27

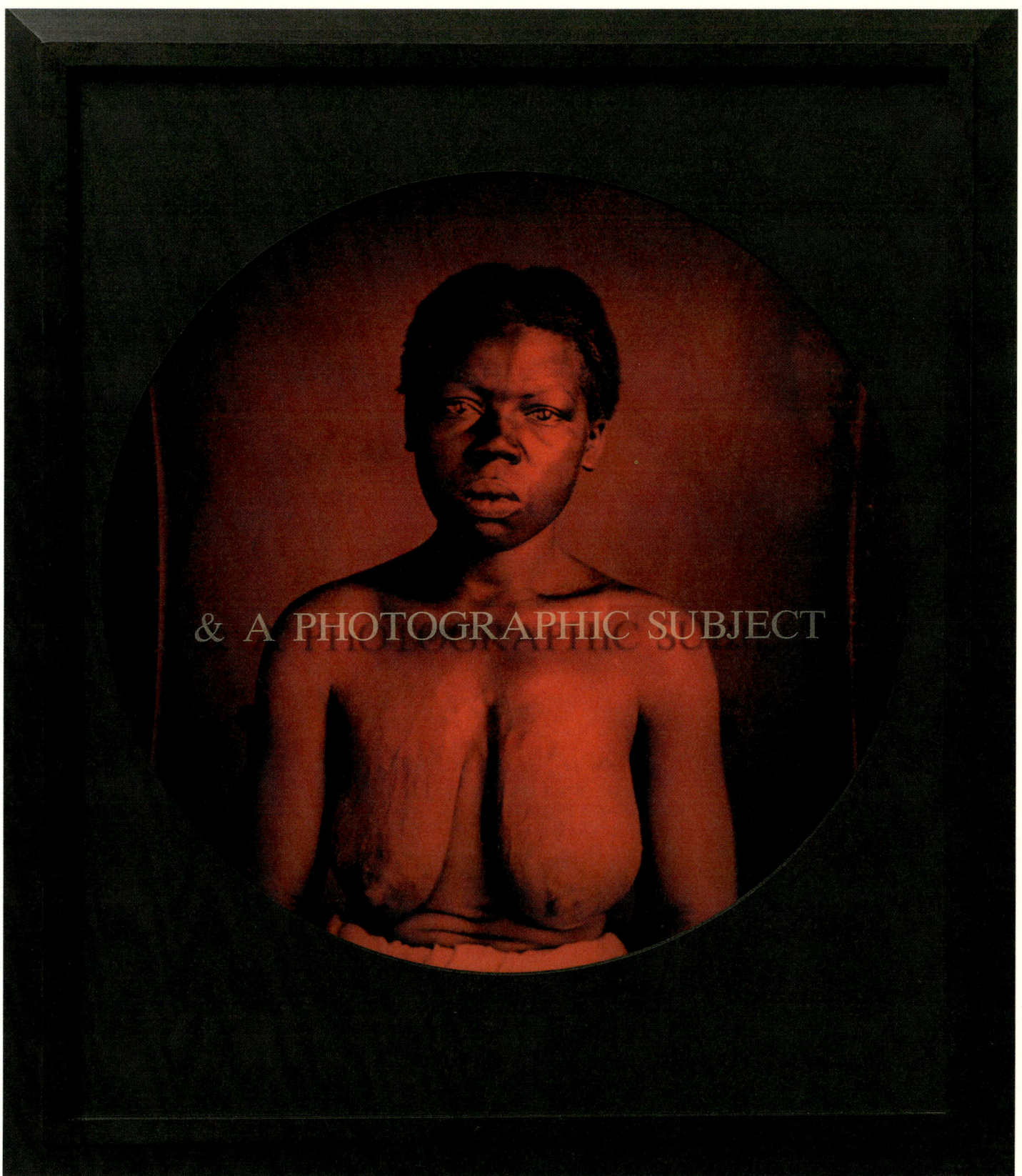

& A PHOTOGRAPHIC SUBJECT

Plate 28

Plate 29

Plate 30

Plate 31

Plate 32

Plate 33

Plate 34

Plate 35

Plate 36

Plate 37

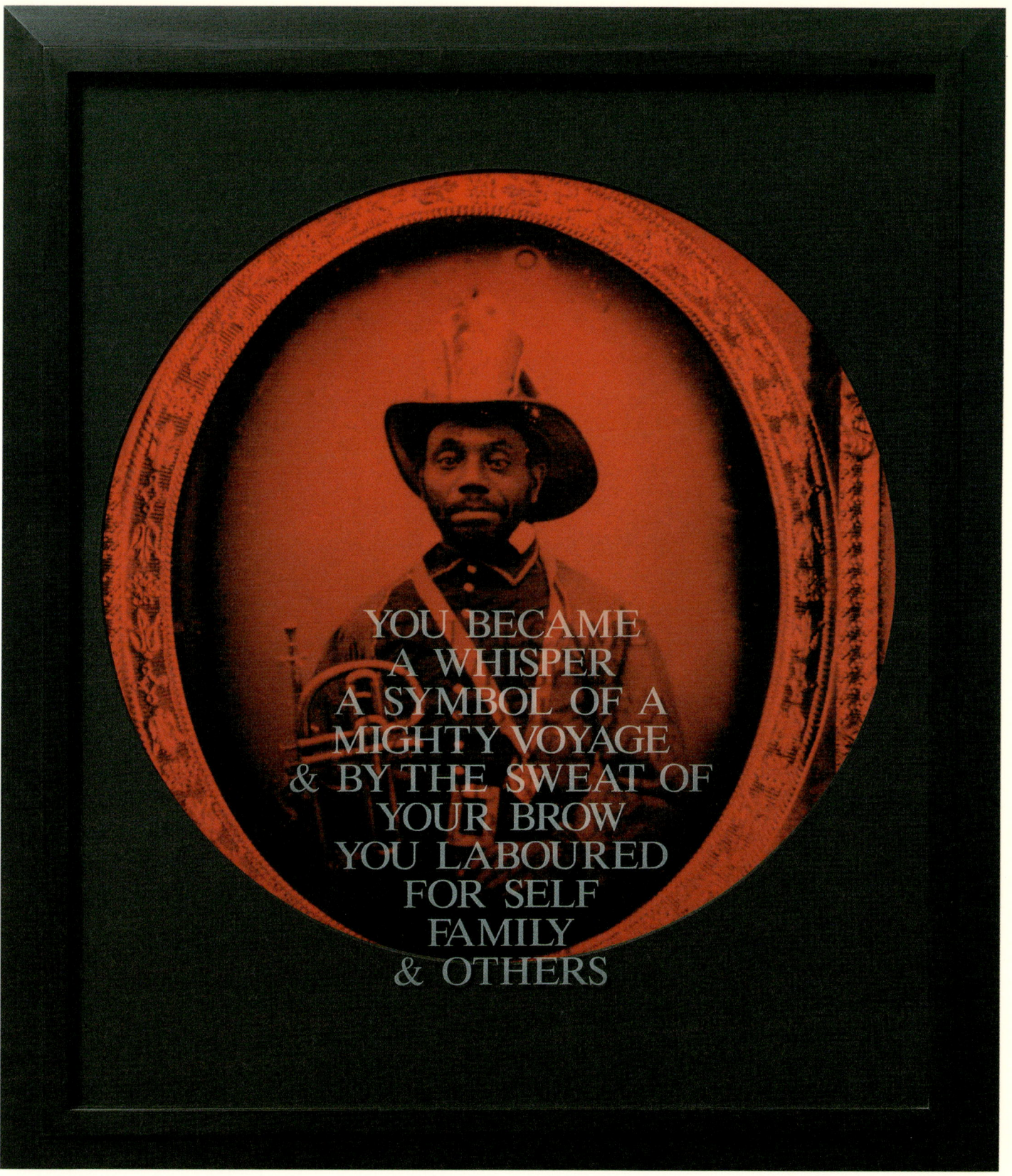

Plate 38

Plate 39

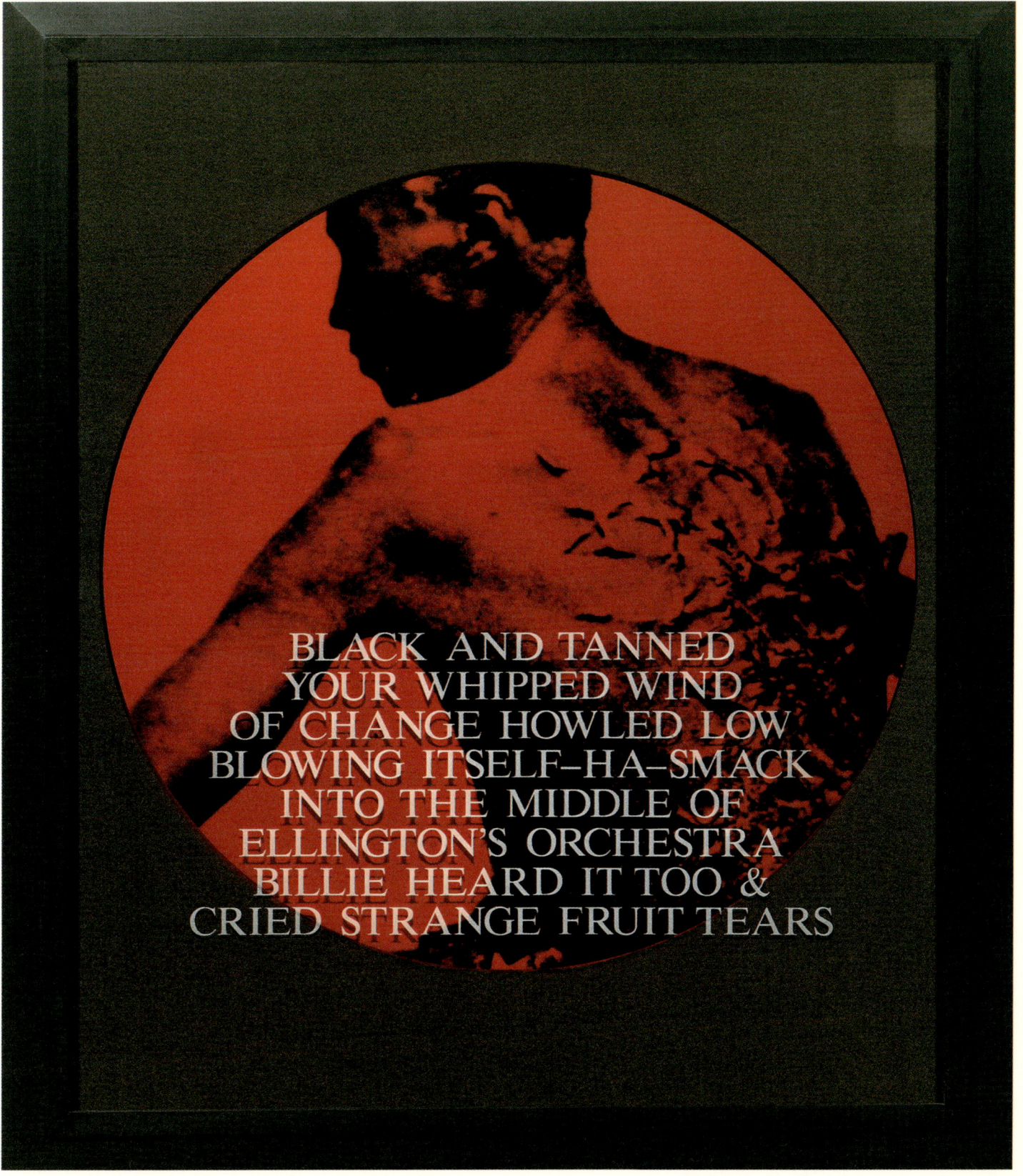

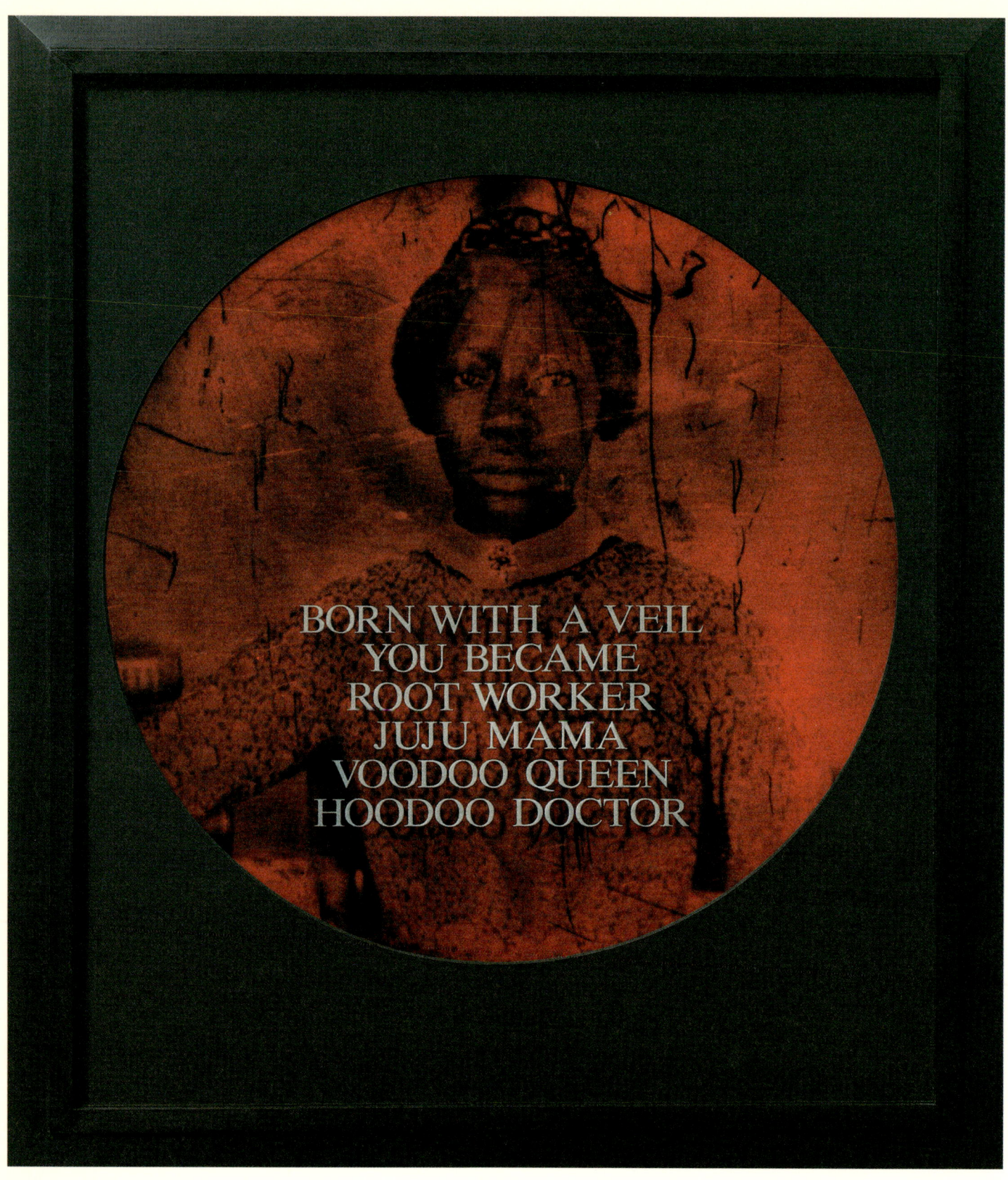

Plate 41

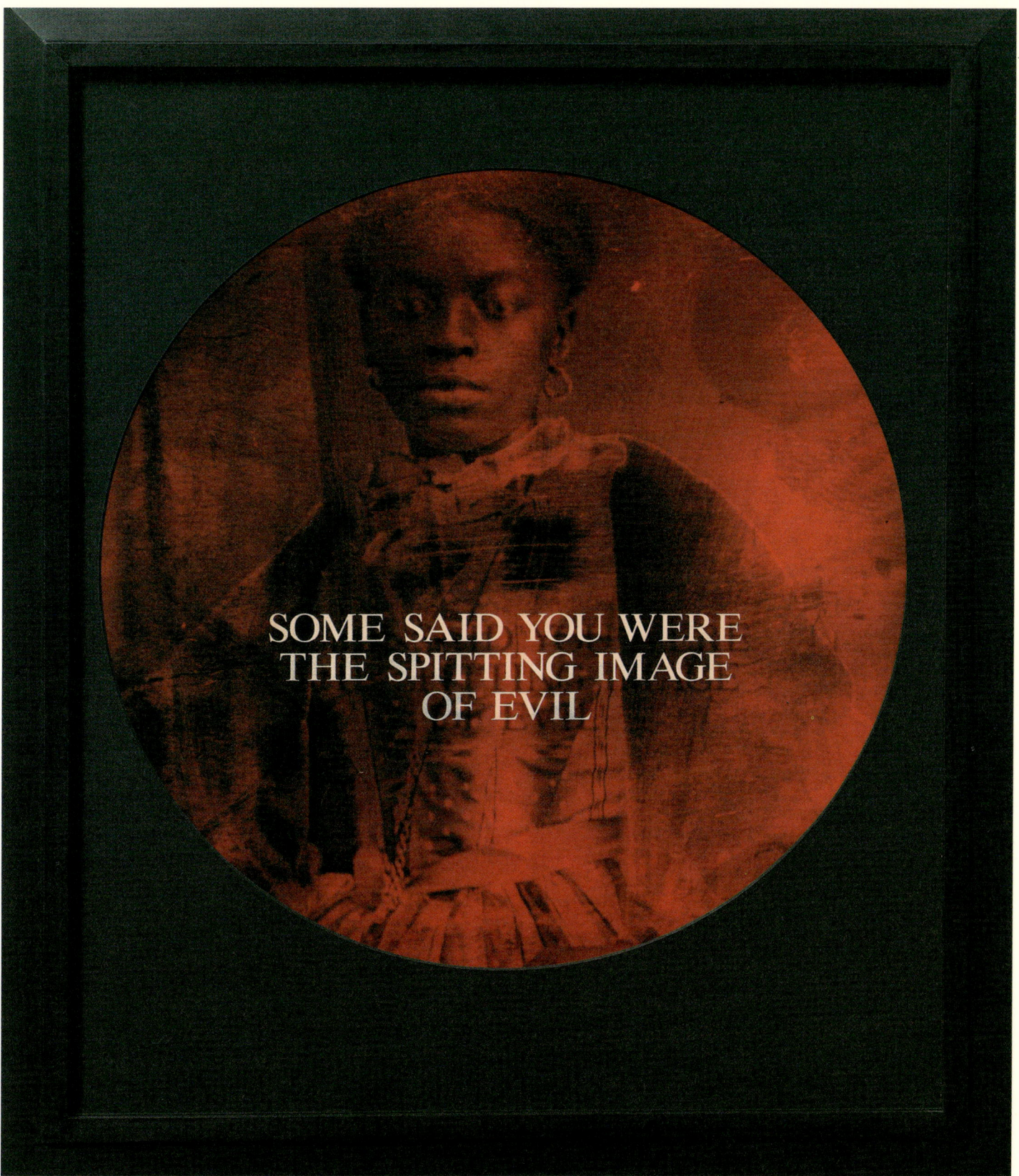

Plate 42

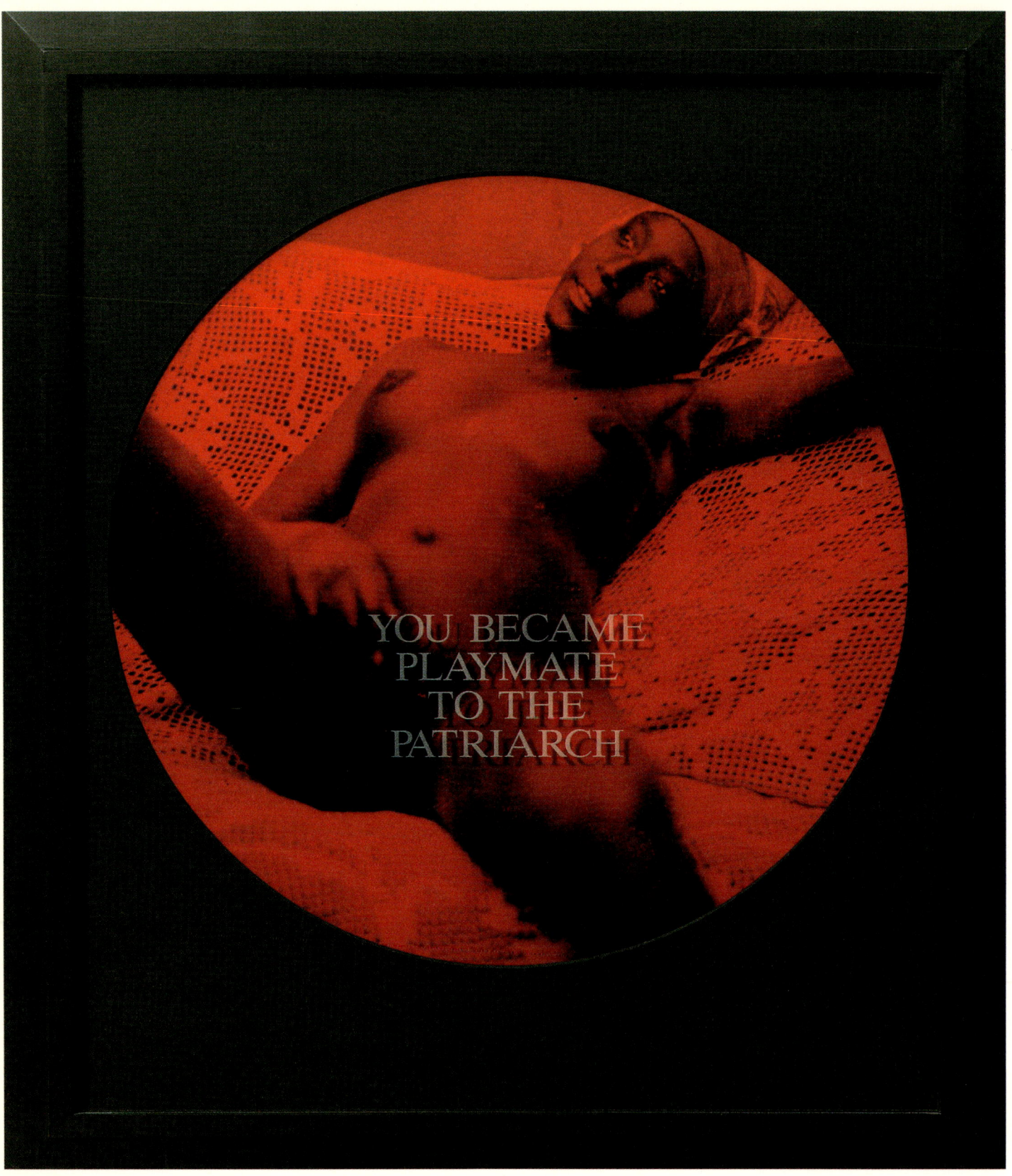

Plate 43

Plate 44

Plate 45

Plate 46

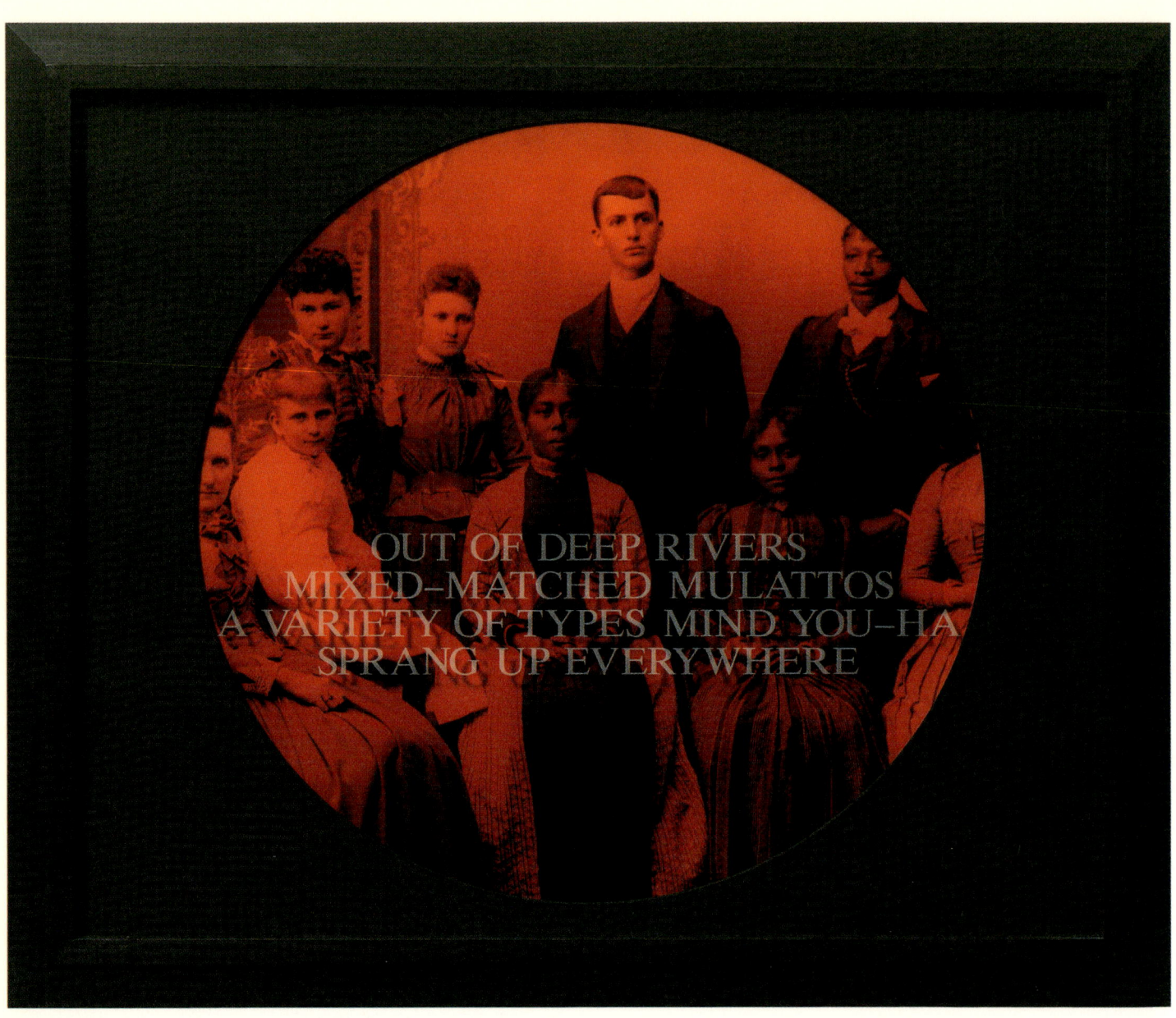

Plate 47

Plate 48

Plate 49

Plate 55

Plate 56

_____WHO WHAT WHEN WHERE
1998

HIP-HIP HOORAY ONCE A

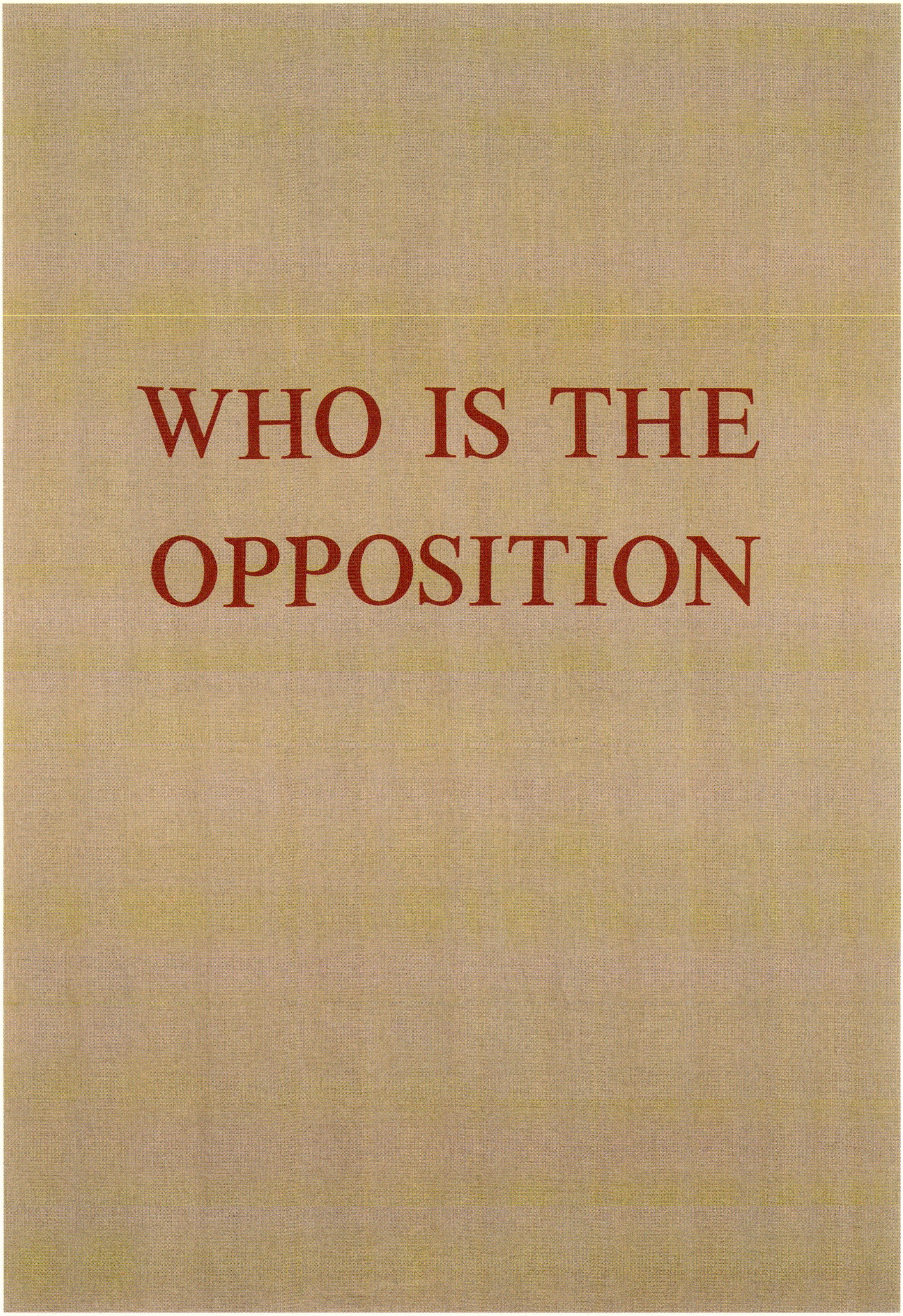

WHO IS THE OPPOSITION

Plate 58

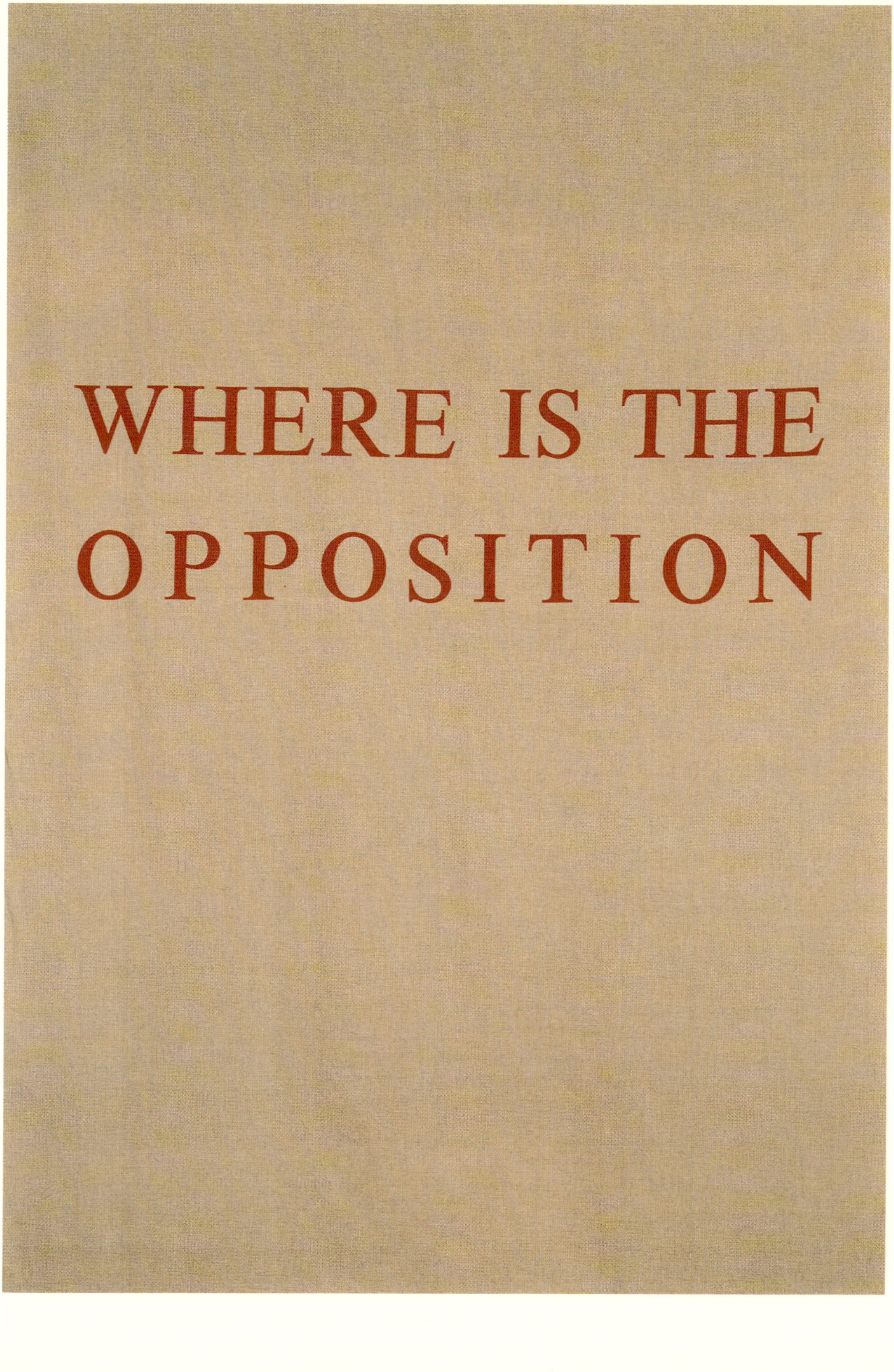

WHERE IS THE OPPOSITION

Plate 59

Plates 60

Plate 62

Plate 63

Plate 64

Plate 65

Plate 66

Plate 67

I REMEMBER LONG NITES AND ENDLESS DISCUSSIONS WITH YOU, WHEN WE WERE NOT AFRAID TO SPEAK OUR MINDS, AND NOW I ONLY FEEL THE HUSH, HUSH, HUSH OF OUR MUTUAL SILENCE.

RITUAL & REVOLUTION

1998

Between the two worlds
I was with you
but as the wind on the Caspian Sea

I was with you
in the ancient ruins of time
you rode me hobby-horse
into the age of revolution

I was with you
when you stormed the Bastille &
The Winter Palace

I was with you
in the hideous mise en scene
of the Middle Passage
One potato, two potato, three potato, four
& in Ireland, too

I was with you
in the death camps
shaved head and all
beating the drummer's drum
shaking in my boots

I was with you
on the longest march
in Cuba & Timbukkta

I was with you
in Santiago
attempting to block
an assassin's bullet
and again in Harlem
cradling Malcolm to my bosom crying

Out of the shadows
from the edge of the new world
I saw your slow persistent emergence &
saw you spinning jenny's cotton into gold

Throughout the course of my existence
& I have been here always
I saw everlasting death
& the endless
weeping of women

I saw you and your father
your mother &
all your sisters
frozen static
in the autumn
of the patriarch

I saw your fear of pleasure
saw you mistaking sexuality for sensuality
& saw your body fragment into a zillion pieces

I saw men and women
locked in a futile struggle for power
& saw the declining significance of race

I saw your hands replaced
by inventions that left you idle
no laurel surrounding your name
no marker to mark
your existence

I saw nor heard any mention of
working, class, you
& you said little
and did even less

In the halls of justice
I spied some of you robbing
the coffers of church & state
smashing the piggy-banks
using the shards
to pick your teeth

I too felt the allure
of temptation's temptress
and in no time flat
saw my own greed
my own corrupt hand
in the pot

Lost for a time
I saw you moving through
the shadowy corridors of
an ageless labyrinth
wondering when and where
it would all end

From the four corners of the world
I saw you bewildered, startled & stumbling
toward the next century
looking over your shoulder
with fingers crossed

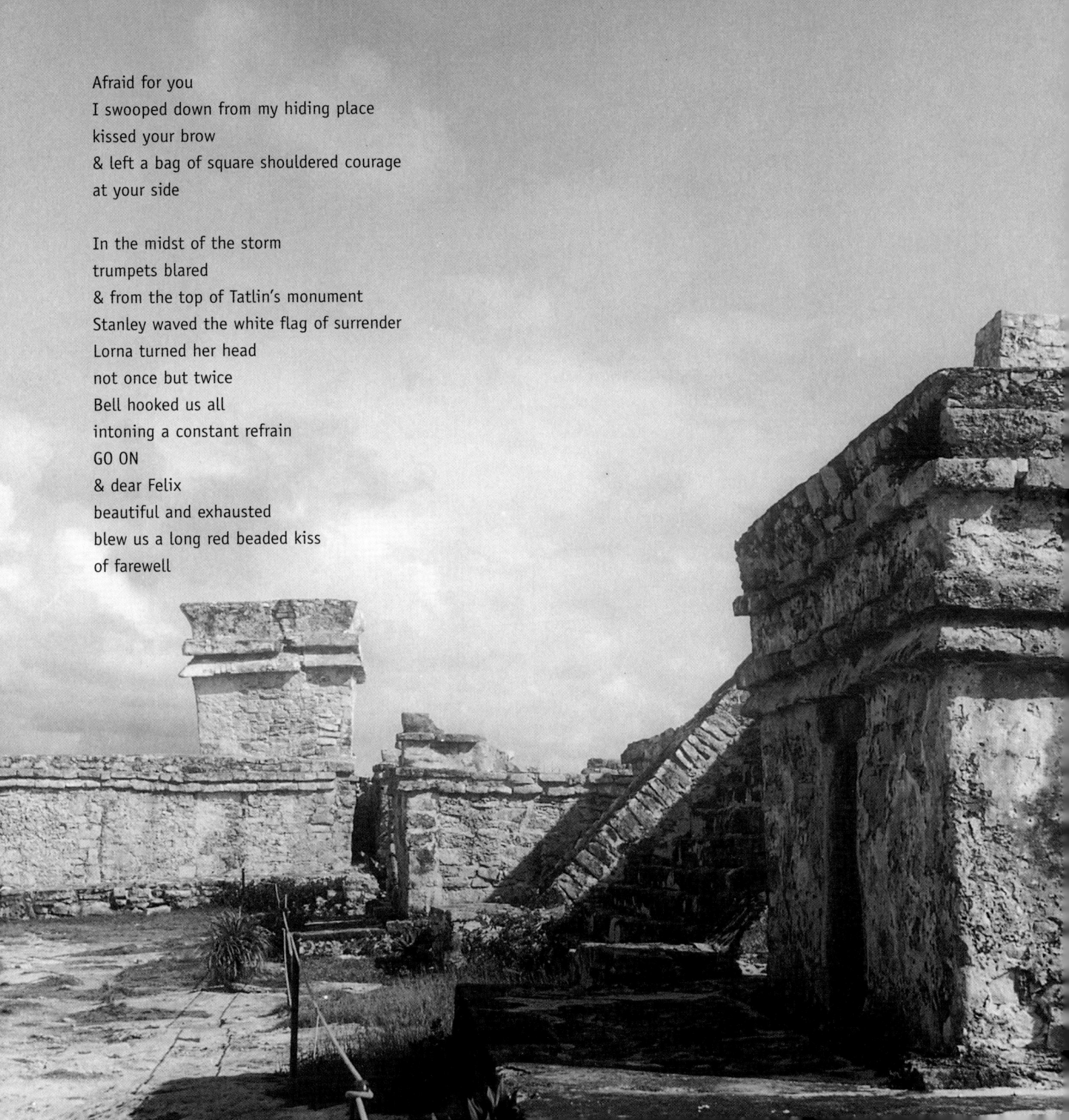

Afraid for you
I swooped down from my hiding place
kissed your brow
& left a bag of square shouldered courage
at your side

In the midst of the storm
trumpets blared
& from the top of Tatlin's monument
Stanley waved the white flag of surrender
Lorna turned her head
not once but twice
Bell hooked us all
intoning a constant refrain
GO ON
& dear Felix
beautiful and exhausted
blew us a long red beaded kiss
of farewell

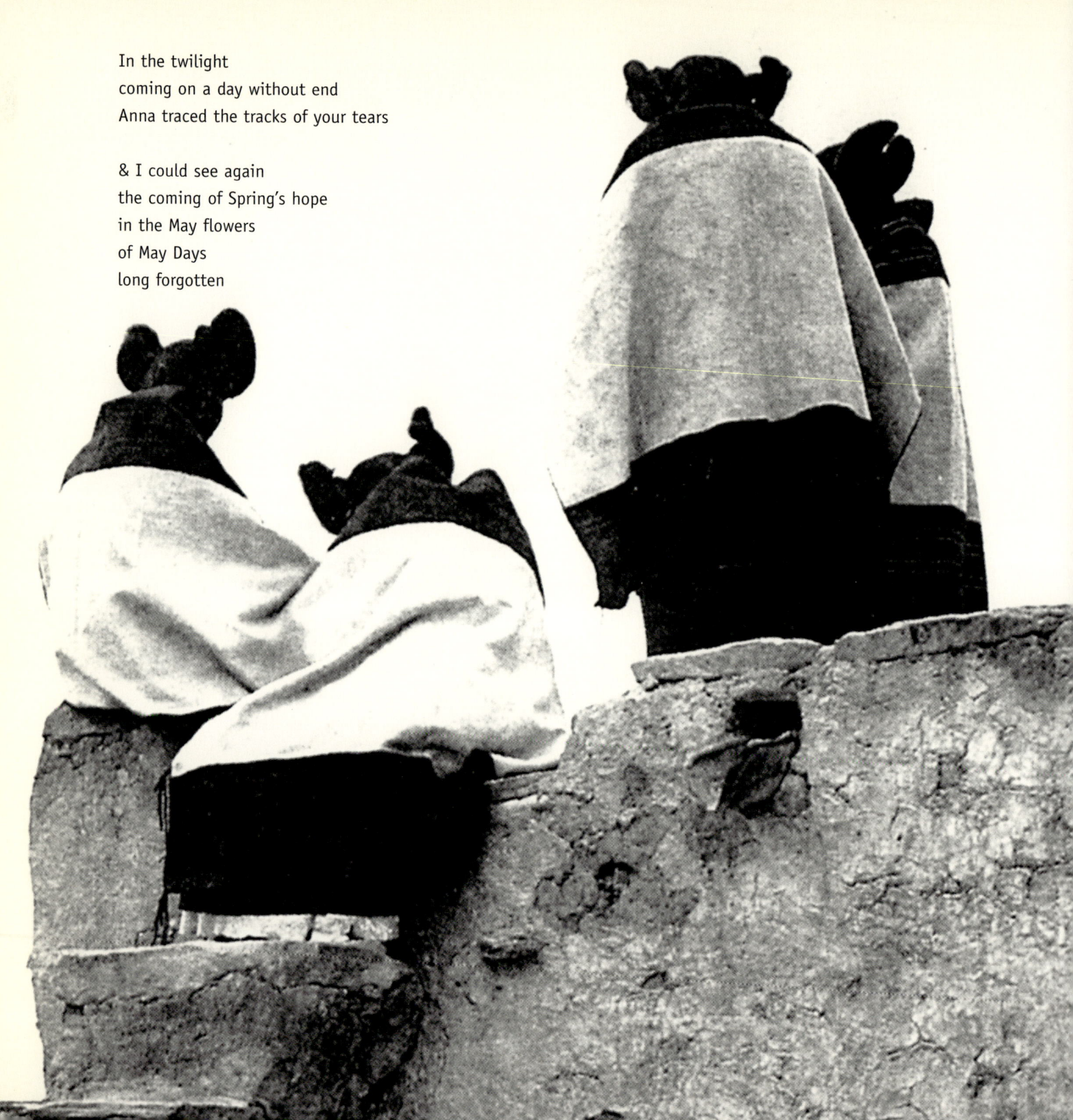

In the twilight
coming on a day without end
Anna traced the tracks of your tears

& I could see again
the coming of Spring's hope
in the May flowers
of May Days
long forgotten

EXHIBITION CHECKLIST

Dimensions are listed in inches, height precedes width, which precedes depth. All works are courtesy of the artist and Pilkington Olsoff Fine Arts, New York, unless otherwise noted.

Sea Islands Series

PLATE 1
Installation of the "Sea Islands Series" at P.P.O.W., N.Y.

PLATE 2
Untitled (Boone Plantation), 1991–92
1 silver print, 1 text panel
Image: 31 x 31
Text panel: 20 x 20

PLATE 3
Untitled (Trailer), 1991–92
detail, right print
2 silver prints
20 x 20 each

PLATE 4
Untitled (Hubcaps), 1991–92
silver print
20 x 20

PLATE 5
Untitled (Ebo Landing), 1991–92
detail, top print
2 silver prints, 1 text panel
20 x 20 each

PLATE 6
Untitled (House), 1991–92
detail, right print
3 silver prints, 1 text panel
20 x 20 each

PLATE 7
Untitled (Boneyard), 1991–92
detail, top print
3 silver prints, 1 text panel
20 x 20 each

PLATE 8
Untitled (Woman in White/Pan of Water), 1991–92
detail, right print
2 silver prints, 2 text panels
20 x 20 each

PLATE 9
Untitled (Woman in White/Pan of Water), 1991–92
detail, left print
2 silver prints, 2 text panels
20 x 20 each

PLATE 10
Untitled (Hat on Bed/Shoes under Bed), 1991–92
detail, top print
2 silver prints
20 x 20

PLATE 11
Untitled (Praise House), 1991–92
detail, right print
2 silver prints
20 x 20

PLATE 12
Untitled (Box Spring in Tree), 1991–92
silver print
20 x 20

Africa Series

PLATE 13
Installation of the "Africa Series" at the Museum of Modern Art, N.Y.

PLATE 14
She Had Her Keys to the Kingdom, 1993
detail, center print
3 C-prints, etched glass
one measures 30 x 30
two measure 30 x 15

PLATE 15
He Had His Throne, 1993
detail, center print
3 C-prints, etched glass
one measures 30 x 30
two measure 30 x 13

PLATE 16
In the Garden, 1993
detail, right print
3 silver prints, 1 text panel
20 x 20 each

PLATE 17
A Place for Him, A Place for Her, 1993
detail, left print
2 silver prints, 2 text panels
20 x 20 each

PLATE 18
The Shape of Things, 1993
detail, center print
3 silver prints
20 x 20 each

PLATE 19
The Shape of Things, 1993
detail, right print
3 silver prints
20 x 20 each

PLATE 20
Untitled, 1993
silver print
20 x 20

PLATE 21
Untitled, 1993
silver print
20 x 20

PLATE 22
Made for Him, Made for Her, 1993
2 C-prints, etched glass
40 x 20 each

PLATE 23
She Was the Apple of Adam's Eye, 1993

pigment and silk embroidery on cotton sateen, with Australian lacewood frame
75 1/4 x 81 1/2 x 1 3/4

From Here I Saw What Happened and I Cried

PLATE 24
From Here I Saw What Happened, 1995–96
C-print with sandblasted text on glass
42 x 31
The Museum of Modern Art, New York
Gift on behalf of The Friends of Education of The Museum of Modern Art

PLATE 25
You Became a Scientific Profile, 1995–96
C-print with sandblasted text on glass
26 3/4 x 22 3/4
From an original daguerreotype taken by J. T. Zealy, 1850. Peabody Museum, Harvard University. Copyright: President & Fellows of Harvard College, 1977. All rights reserved.
The Museum of Modern Art, New York
Gift on behalf of The Friends of Education of The Museum of Modern Art

PLATE 26
A Negroid Type, 1995–96
C-print with sandblasted text on glass
26 3/4 x 22 3/4
From an original daguerreotype taken by J. T. Zealy, 1850. Peabody Museum, Harvard University. Copyright: President & Fellows of Harvard College, 1977. All rights reserved.
The Museum of Modern Art, New York
Gift on behalf of The Friends of Education of The Museum of Modern Art

PLATE 27
An Anthropological Debate, 1995–96
C-print with sandblasted text on glass
26 3/4 x 22 3/4
From an original daguerreotype taken by J. T. Zealy, 1850. Peabody Museum, Harvard University. Copyright: President & Fellows of Harvard College, 1977. All rights reserved.
The Museum of Modern Art, New York
Gift on behalf of The Friends of Education of The Museum of Modern Art

PLATE 28
& A Photographic Subject, 1995–96
C-print with sandblasted text on glass
26 3/4 x 22 3/4
From an original daguerreotype taken by J. T. Zealy, 1850. Peabody Museum, Harvard University. Copyright: President & Fellows of Harvard College, 1977. All rights reserved.
The Museum of Modern Art, New York
Gift on behalf of The Friends of Education of The Museum of Modern Art

PLATE 29
You Became Mammie, Mama, Mother & Then, Yes, Confidant—Ha, 1995–96
C-print with sandblasted text on glass
26 3/4 x 22 3/4
The Museum of Modern Art, New York
Gift on behalf of The Friends of Education of The Museum of Modern Art

PLATE 30
Descending the Throne You Became Foot Soldier & Cook, 1995–96
C-print with sandblasted text on glass
26 3/4 x 22 3/4
The Museum of Modern Art, New York
Gift on behalf of The Friends of Education of The Museum of Modern Art

PLATE 31
House, 1995–96
C-print with sandblasted text on glass
26 3/4 x 22 3/4
The Museum of Modern Art, New York
Gift on behalf of The Friends of Education of The Museum of Modern Art

PLATE 32
Yard, 1995–96
C-print with sandblasted text on glass
26 3/4 x 22 3/4
The Museum of Modern Art, New York
Gift on behalf of The Friends of Education of The Museum of Modern Art

PLATE 33
Field, 1995–96
C-print with sandblasted text on glass
26 3/4 x 22 3/4
The Museum of Modern Art, New York
Gift on behalf of The Friends of Education of The Museum of Modern Art

PLATE 34
Kitchen, 1995–96
C-print with sandblasted text on glass
26 3/4 x 22 3/4
The Museum of Modern Art, New York
Gift on behalf of The Friends of Education of The Museum of Modern Art

PLATE 35
You Became Uncle Tom, John & Clemens' Jim, 1995–96
C-print with sandblasted text on glass
26 3/4 x 22 3/4
The Museum of Modern Art, New York
Gift on behalf of The Friends of Education of The Museum of Modern Art

PLATE 36
Drivers, 1995–96
C-print with sandblasted text on glass
26 3/4 x 22 3/4
The Museum of Modern Art, New York
Gift on behalf of The Friends of Education of The Museum of Modern Art

PLATE 37
Riders & Men of Letters, 1995–96
C-print with sandblasted text on glass
26 3/4 x 22 3/4
The Museum of Modern Art, New York
Gift on behalf of The Friends of Education of The Museum of Modern Art

PLATE 38
You Became a Whisper, a Symbol of a Mighty Voyage & By the Sweat of Your Brow You Laboured for Self, Family & Others, 1995–96
C-print with sandblasted text on glass
26 3/4 x 22 3/4
The Museum of Modern Art, New York
Gift on behalf of The Friends of Education of The Museum of Modern Art

PLATE 39
For Your Names You Took Hope & Humble, 1995–96
C-print with sandblasted text on glass
26 3/4 x 22 3/4
The Museum of Modern Art, New York
Gift on behalf of The Friends of Education of The Museum of Modern Art

PLATE 40
Black and Tanned Your Whipped Wind of

*Change Howled Low Blowing Itself—Ha—
Smack into the Middle of Ellington's
Orchestra Billie Heard It Too & Cried Strange
Fruit Tears,* 1995–96
C-print with sandblasted text on glass
26 3/4 x 22 3/4
The Museum of Modern Art, New York
Gift on behalf of The Friends of Education
of The Museum of Modern Art

PLATE 41
*Born with a Veil You Became Root Worker,
Juju Mama, Voodoo Queen, Hoodoo Doctor,*
1995–96
C-print with sandblasted text on glass
26 3/4 x 22 3/4
The Museum of Modern Art, New York
Gift on behalf of The Friends of Education
of The Museum of Modern Art

PLATE 42
*Some Said You Were the Spitting Image of
Evil,* 1995–96
C-print with sandblasted text on glass
26 3/4 x 22 3/4
The Museum of Modern Art, New York
Gift on behalf of The Friends of Education
of The Museum of Modern Art

PLATE 43
You Became Playmate to the Patriarch,
1995–96
C-print with sandblasted text on glass
26 3/4 x 22 3/4
The Museum of Modern Art, New York
Gift on behalf of The Friends of Education
of The Museum of Modern Art

PLATE 44
And Their Daughter, 1995–96
C-print with sandblasted text on glass
26 3/4 x 22 3/4
The Museum of Modern Art, New York
Gift on behalf of The Friends of Education
of The Museum of Modern Art

PLATE 45
You Became an Accomplice, 1995–96
C-print with sandblasted text on glass
26 3/4 x 22 3/4

PLATE 46
God Bless the Child, 1995–96
C-print with sandblasted text on glass
26 3/4 x 22 3/4
The Museum of Modern Art, New York
Gift on behalf of The Friends of Education
of The Museum of Modern Art

PLATE 47
*Out of Deep Rivers Mixed-Matched Mulattos
a Variety of Types Mind You—Ha—Sprang
Up Everywhere,* 1995–96
C-print with sandblasted text on glass
22 3/4 x 26 3/4
The Museum of Modern Art, New York
Gift on behalf of The Friends of Education
of The Museum of Modern Art

PLATE 48
*Your Resistance Was Found in the Food
You Placed on the Master's Table—Ha,*
1995–96
C-print with sandblasted text on glass
22 3/4 x 26 3/4
The Museum of Modern Art, New York
Gift on behalf of The Friends of Education
of The Museum of Modern Art

PLATE 49
You Became the Joker's Joke &, 1995–96
C-print with sandblasted text on glass
26 3/4 x 22 3/4
The Museum of Modern Art, New York
Gift on behalf of The Friends of Education
of The Museum of Modern Art

PLATE 50
Anything but What You Were Ha,
1995–96
C-print with sandblasted text on glass
26 3/4 x 22 3/4

PLATE 51
Some Laughed Long & Hard & Loud,
1995–96
C-print with sandblasted text on glass
22 3/4 x 26 3/4
The Museum of Modern Art, New York
Gift on behalf of The Friends of Education
of The Museum of Modern Art

PLATE 52
*Others Said 'Only Thing a Niggah Could Do
Was Shine My Shoes,'* 1995–96
C-print with sandblasted text on glass
22 3/4 x 26 3/4

PLATE 53
You Became Boots, Spades & Coons,
1995–96
C-print with sandblasted text on glass
26 3/4 x 22 3/4
The Museum of Modern Art, New York
Gift on behalf of The Friends of Education
of The Museum of Modern Art

PLATE 54
*Restless After the Longest Winter You
Marched & Marched & Marched,* 1995–96
C-print with sandblasted text on glass
26 3/4 x 22 3/4
The Museum of Modern Art, New York
Gift on behalf of The Friends of Education
of The Museum of Modern Art

PLATE 55
*In Your Sing Song Prayer You Asked Didn't
My Lord Deliver Daniel?,* 1995–96
C-print with sandblasted text on glass
26 3/4 x 22 3/4
The Museum of Modern Art, New York
Gift on behalf of The Friends of Education
of The Museum of Modern Art

PLATE 56
And I Cried, 1995–96
C-print with sandblasted text on glass
26 3/4 x 22 3/4
The Museum of Modern Art, New York
Gift on behalf of The Friends of Education
of The Museum of Modern Art

Who What When Where

PLATE 57
Saving Capital, 1998
digital photo on canvas, color pigment
120 x 240

PLATE 58
Who Is the Opposition, 1998
digital photo on canvas, color pigment
96 x 60

PLATE 59
Where Is the Opposition, 1998
digital photo on canvas, color pigment
96 x 60

PLATE 60
Who, 1998
digital photo on canvas, color pigment
84 x 66

PLATE 61
What, 1998
digital photo on canvas, color pigment
84 x 66

PLATE 62
When, 1998
digital photo on canvas, color pigment
84 x 66

PLATE 63
Where, 1998
digital photo on canvas, color pigment
84 x 66

PLATE 64
Red Square or Position of Native Peoples, 1998
digital photo on canvas, color pigment
56 x 72 ½

PLATE 65
Sometimes a Great Notion, 1998
cherry wood
120 x 48 x 48

PLATE 66
Tatlin's Monument for the Future, 1998
steel
74 x 66 x 87

PLATE 67
Black Square or Dancing in Congo Square, 1998
digital photo on canvas, color pigment
56 x 72 ½

PLATE 68
The Hush of Your Silence, 1998
digital photo on canvas, color pigment
84 x 66

Ritual & Revolution

PLATE 69
Installation of "Ritual & Revolution" at P.P.O.W., N.Y.

PLATES 70–81
"Ritual & Revolution," 1998
digital photos on muslin, color pigment
12 banners, variable dimensions, audio component

PHOTO CREDITS
D. James Dee: plates 13–15, 22, 25–30, 35–38, 41–45, 47–49, 51, 53–55, 58–63, and 66

The J. Paul Getty Museum, Los Angeles: plates 24, 31–34, 39, 40, 50, 52, and 56

John Morris: plates 64, 65, 67, and 68

Adam Reich: plates 1 and 69

Fred Scruton: plate 46

Will Brown: plate 23

BIOGRAPHY

1953   Born in Portland, Oregon

Education

1981   BFA, California Institute of the Arts, Valencia, Calif.

1984   MFA, University of California at San Diego, Calif.

1984–87   Graduate Program in Folklore, University of California, Berkeley, Calif.

Teaching

1983–84   Teaching Assistant, University of California at San Diego, Calif.

1984   Teacher, San Diego City College, San Diego, Calif.

1985–86   Folklife Program-Festival at the Lake, Oakland, Calif.

1987   Teaching Assistant, University of California at Berkeley, Berkeley, Calif.

1987–91   Assistant Professor, Hampshire College, Amherst, Mass.

1988–89   Visiting Professor, Hunter College, New York, N.Y.

1991   Assistant Professor, California College of the Arts & Crafts, Oakland, Calif.

Solo Shows

1984   "Family Pictures and Stories," Multi-Cultural Gallery, San Diego, Calif.

          "Family Pictures and Stories: A Photographic Installation," Alternative Space Gallery, San Diego, Calif.

1987   Hampshire College Art Gallery, Amherst, Mass.

1989   Red Eye Gallery, Rhode Island School of Design, Providence, R.I.

1990   "Calling Out My Name," Center for Exploratory and Perceptual Art, Buffalo, N.Y., P.P.O.W., New York, N.Y.

1991   "Currents: Carrie Mae Weems," Institute of Contemporary Art, Boston, Mass.

          Trustman Gallery, Simmons College, Boston, Mass.

          "And 22 Million Very Tired and Very Angry People," The New Museum of Contemporary Art, New York, N.Y.

          Matrix Gallery, Wadsworth Atheneum, Hartford, Conn.

          "Family Pictures and Stories," curated by Perry Nesbitt, Albright College, Freedman Gallery, Reading, Pa.

          "Carrie Mae Weems: Two Works," curated by Phylis Lutjeans, University of Southern California at Irvine, Calif.

          "Family Pictures and Stories," curated by Wendy Kaplan, Art Complex Museum, Duxbury, Mass.

1992   Greenville County Museum of Art, Greenville, S.C.

"And 22 Million Very Tired and Very Angry People," Walter/McBean Gallery, San Francisco Art Institute, San Francisco, Calif.

"Sea Islands Series," P.P.O.W., New York, N.Y.

"Family Pictures and Stories," Cleveland Center for Contemporary Art, Cleveland, Ohio

"Installation," Nexus Contemporary Art Center, Atlanta, Ga., in conjunction with New Langton Arts, San Francisco, Calif.

1993 "Sea Islands Series," Linda Cathcart Gallery, Santa Monica, Calif.

"Sea Islands Series," Rhona Hoffman Gallery, Chicago, Ill.

New Langton Arts, San Francisco, Calif.

The Fabric Workshop, Philadelphia, Pa.

"Carrie Mae Weems: Recent Works," P.P.O.W., New York, N.Y.

1993–94 "Carrie Mae Weems," curated by Andrea Kish and Susan Fisher Sterling. Traveling to: The National Museum of Women in the Arts, Washington D.C.; Forum for Contemporary Art, St. Louis, Mo.; Museum of Modern Art, San Francisco, Calif.; Afro-American Museum, Los Angeles, Calif.; Contemporary Arts Center, Cincinnati, Ohio; Center for the Fine Arts, Miami, Fla.; Walker Art Center, Minneapolis, Minn.; Portland Art Museum, Portland Oreg.; and the Institute of Contemporary Art, Philadelphia, Pa.

1994 Dartmouth College, Hood Museum of Art, Hanover, N.H.

"Carrie Mae Weems," Dakar Biennial, Dakar, Senegal

1994–95 "In These Islands, South Carolina, Georgia." Traveling exhibition organized by William Dooley, University of Alabama, Sarah Moody Gallery of Art, Tuscaloosa, Ala.; Northern Illinois University, NIU Art Museum, Dekalb, Ill.; Southern Oregon State College, Schneider Museum of Art, Ashland, Oreg.; University of South Carolina, McKissick Museum, Columbia, S.C.; University of Iowa, Museum of Art, Iowa City, Iowa

1995 "Carrie Mae Weems Reacts to Hidden Witness," The J. Paul Getty Museum, Malibu, Calif.

Projects 52, Museum of Modern Art, New York, N.Y.

1996 "From Here I Saw What Happened and I Cried," P.P.O.W., New York, N.Y.

"Carrie Mae Weems: The Kitchen Table Series," Contemporary Arts Museum, Houston, Tex.

"From Here I Saw What Happened and I Cried," Rhona Hoffman Gallery, Chicago, Ill.

"Sea Islands Series," and "Africa Series," University of Illinois, Krannert Art Museum, Champaign, Ill.

"From Here I Saw What Happened and I Cried," Gallery Paule Anglim, San Francisco, Calif.

"From Here I Saw What Happened and I Cried," The Bunting Institute, Cambridge, Mass.

1997 2nd Johannesburg Biennial, Africus Institute for Contemporary Art, Johannesburg, South Africa

"Africa Series," Virginia Museum of Fine Arts, Richmond, Va.

Cline LewAllen Contemporary, Santa Fe, N.M.

Three Rivers Festival, Philadelphia, Pa.

1998 "Who What When Where," The Whitney Museum of American Art at Philip Morris, New York, N.Y.

"Ritual & Revolution," DAK'ART 98: Biennial of Contemporary Art, Galerie Nationale d'Art, Dakar, Senegal

"Ritual & Revolution," P.P.O.W., New York, N.Y.

"Ritual & Revolution," University of California, Berkeley Art Museum and Pacific Film Archive, Berkeley, Calif.

Recent Works, Künstlerhaus Bethanien, Berlin, Germany

Harriet Tubman Museum of Art, Macon, Ga.

1998–99 "Carrie Mae Weems: Recent Work, 1992–1998," Everson Museum of Art, Syracuse, N.Y.

Selected Group Shows

1980 "Contemporary Black Photographers," San Francisco State University, San Francisco, Calif.

"Black Artists in Los Angeles," Brockman Gallery, Los Angeles, Calif.

1981 "Multi-Cultural Focus," Barnsdall Art Gallery, Los Angeles, Calif.

"Women in Photography," Cityscape Foto Gallery, Pasadena, Calif.

1983 "Four West Coast Photographers," Vanderbilt University Art Gallery, Nashville, Tenn.

"Dropped Lines," Center for Women's Studies and Services, San Diego, Calif.

1985 "Analysis and Passion: Photography Engages Social and Political Issues," Eye Gallery, San Francisco, Calif.

1986 "Relations," Los Angeles Center for Photographic Studies, Los Angeles, Calif.

"America: Another Perspective," Grey Art Gallery and Study Center, New York University, N.Y.

"Past, Present, Future," New Museum for Contemporary Art, New York, N.Y.

1987 "Edict and Episode: Image as Meaning," Installation Gallery, San Diego, Calif.

"Photographs by Hilton Braithwaite and Carrie Mae Weems," Hampshire College Art Gallery, Amherst, Mass.

1988 "The Other," The Houston Center for Photography, Houston, Tex.

"Herstory: Black Women Photographers," Firehouse Gallery, Houston, Tex.

"Prisoners of Image, 1800–1988," Alternative Museum, New York, N.Y.

1989 "A Century of Protest," traveling exhibition, Williams College Museum of Art, Williamstown, Mass.

"Self Portrayals," University Art Museum, State University of New York at Binghamton, N.Y.

"Black Photographers Bear Witness: 100 Years of Social Protest," traveling exhibition, Williams College Museum of Art, Williamstown, Mass.

"Prisoners of Image Ethnic and Gender Stereotypes," Alternative Museum, New York, N.Y.

1990 "Black Women Photographers," Ten-8, London

"Recent Works," CEPA Gallery, Buffalo, N.Y.

"Cultural Diversity," Southern Illinois University, University Museum, Carbondale, Ill.

"The Power of Words: Aspects of Recent Documentary Photography," P.P.O.W., New York, N.Y.

"Urban Home," Studio Museum in Harlem, New York, N.Y.

"Spent: Currency, Security, and Art on Deposit," Marine Midland Bank, in conjunction with New Museum of Contemporary Art, New York, N.Y.

"The Empire's New Clothes," Camerawork, London, UK

1991 "Reframing the Family," Artists Space, New York, N.Y.

"Carrie Mae Weems and Jeffrey Hoone," Camerawork, London, UK

"Currents," Institute of Contemporary Photography, Boston, Mass.

"Whitney Biennial," Whitney Museum of American Art, New York, N.Y.

"Sexuality, Image and Control," Houston Center for Photography, Houston, Tex.

"The Art of Advocacy," Aldrich Museum of Contemporary Art, Ridgefield, Conn.

"Pleasures and Terrors of Domestic Comfort," curated by Peter Galassi, The Museum of Modern Art, New York, N.Y., traveling to Baltimore Museum of Art, Baltimore, Md.; Los Angeles County Museum of Art, Los Angeles, Calif.; The Contemporary Arts Center, Cincinnati, Ohio

1991–92 "Artists of Conscience: 16 Years of Social and Political Commentary," Alternative Museum, New York, N.Y.

1991–93 "No Laughing Matter," curated by Nina Felshin, University of North Texas, Denton, Tex.; Alberta College Art Gallery, Calgary, Alberta, Canada; Art Gallery, Halifax, Nova Scotia, Canada; University of Nebraska, Sheldon Memorial Art Gallery and Sculpture Garden, Lincoln, Nebr.; Tufts University Art Gallery, Medford, Mass.

1992 "Schwarze Kunst: Konzepte zur Politik und Identität," Neue Gesellschaft für bildende Kunst, Berlin, Germany

"Dirt and Domesticity: Construction of the Feminine," Whitney Museum of American Art at Equitable Center, New York, N.Y.

"Family Pictures and Stories," Cleveland Center for Contemporary Art, Cleveland, Ohio

"Representatives: Women Photographers from the Permanent Collection," Center for Creative Photography, The University of Arizona, Tucson, Ariz.

"Empowering the Viewer: Art, Politics and Community," curated by Don Desmett, William Benton Museum of Art, University of Connecticut, Storrs, Conn.; Temple Gallery, Temple University, Philadelphia, Pa.; Tyler Gallery, Tyler School of Art, Temple University, Elkins Park, Pa.

"Between the Sheets," P.P.O.W., New York, N.Y.

1992–94 "Mis/Taken Identities," curated by Abigail Solomon-Godeau and Constance Lewallen, University of California, Santa Barbara Art Museum, traveling to Museum Folkwang, Essen, Germany; Forum Stadtpark, Graz, Austria; Neues Museum Weserburg Bremen im Forum Langenstraße, Germany; Louisiana Museum of Modern Art, Humlebaek, Denmark; Western Gallery, Western Washington University, Bellingham, Wash.

"Photography: Expanding the Collection," Whitney Museum of American Art, New York, N.Y.

1993 "There Is a World Through Our Eyes: Expanding the Boundaries of Spirituality, Belief and Movement," Rockland Center for the Arts, Nyack, N.Y.

"1920: The Subtlety of Subversion/The Continuity of Intervertion," Exit Art/The First World, New York, N.Y.

"Personal Narratives," Southeastern Center for Contemporary Art, Winston-Salem, N.C.

1993–94 "The Theater of Refusal: Black Art and the Mainstream Criticism," curated by Charles Gaines traveling to University of California, Irvine, The Art Gallery; University of California, Davis, Richard L. Nelson Gallery & The Fine Arts Collection; University of California, Riverside, Museum of Photography

1994 "Gesture and Pose," The Museum of Modern Art, New York, N.Y.

"Bad Girls, Part 1," curated by Marcia Tanner and Marcia Tucker, New Museum of Contemporary Art, New York, N.Y.

"Existence and Gender: Women's Representation of Women," Sapporo American Center Gallery, Sapporo, Japan. Traveled to Aka Renga Cultural Center, Fukuoka City, Japan; Kyoto International Community House, Kyoto, Japan; Aichi Prefectural Arts Center, Nagoya, Japan; Osaka Perfectural Contemporary Arts Center, Tokyo, Japan.

"Who's Looking at the Family?" curated by Carol Brown, Barbican Art Gallery, Barbican Centre, London, UK

1994–95 "Imagining Families: Images and Voices," curated by Deborah Willis, The Smithsonian Institution, Washington, D.C.

"Black Male, Representations of Masculinity in Contemporary American Art," curated by Thelma Golden, Whitney Museum of American Art, New York, N.Y., and The Armand Hammer Musuem of Art, Santa Monica, Calif.

1995 "95 Kwangju Biennial," Seoul, Korea

"Storyland: Narrative Vision and Social Space," Walter Phillips Gallery, The Banff Center for the Arts, Banff, Canada

1996 "Bearing Witness: Contemporary Works by African-American Artists," Spellman College Museum of Fine Art, Spellman College, Atlanta, Ga.

"Inside the Visible," Institute of Contemporary Art, Boston, Mass.; The National Museum of Women in the Arts, Washington, D.C.; international traveling exhibition

"Herkunft," Winterthur Fotomuseum, curated by Urs Stabel, Winterthur, Switzerland

"Gender-Beyond Memory," curated by Michiko Kasahara, Tokyo Metropolitan Museum of Photography, Tokyo, Japan

"From Here I Saw What Happened and I Cried," Biennale Firenze 96, Florence, Italy

"Inclusion/Exclusion," Steirischer Herbst, Graz, Austria

"Tragic Wake: The Legacy of Slavery and the African Diaspora in Contemporary American Art," Spirit Square Center for Arts and Education, Charlotte, N.C.

1997 "Alternating Currents," the Johannesburg Biennial, Johannesburg, South Africa

"Making Pictures: Women and Photography, 1975–Now," Bernard Toale Gallery, Boston, Mass.

"Four Decades," P.P.O.W., New York, N.Y.

"No Small Feat," Rhona Hoffman Gallery, Chicago, Ill.

"Original Visions: Women, Art and the Politics of Gender," Boston College Museum of Art, Boston, Mass.

"dislocations/siirtymiä," Rovaniemi Art Museum, Finland

1997–98 "Changing Spaces," The Detroit Institute of Arts, Detroit, Mich.

1998 "Bearing Witness: Contemporary Works by African-American Artists," Polk Museum of Art, Lakeland, Fla.; Columbus Museum, Columbus, Ga.; African American Museum, Dallas, Tex.; Minnesota Museum of American Art, St. Paul, Minn.

"Years Ending in Nine," The Museum of Fine Arts, Houston, Tex.

"Taboo: Repression and Revolt in Modern Art," Galerie St. Etienne, New York, N.Y.

"Tell Me a Story: Narration in Contemporary Painting and Photography," Centre National d'Art Contemporain de Grenoble, Grenoble, France

"Claustrophobia: Disturbing the Domestic in Contemporary Art," Ikon Gallery, Birmingham, UK

"Roots & Reeds: The Amazing Grace of the Gullah People," Hunter College, New York, N.Y.

1999 "Bearing Witness: Contemporary Works by African-American Artists," Gibbes Museum of Art, Charleston, S.C.; Edwin A. Ulrich Museum of Art, Wichita State University, Wichita, Kans.; Portland Museum of Art, Portland, Maine; Museum of Fine Arts, Houston, Tex.; African-American History and Cultural Museum, Fresno, Calif.

Awards, Grants, and Residencies

1981 Los Angeles Women's Building Poster Award

1981–85 University of California Fellowship Award

1982 University of California Chancellor's Grant

1983 California Arts Council Grant

1986 Artist in Residence, Visual Studies Workshop, Rochester, N.Y.

1987 Smithsonian Fellow, Smithsonian Institution, Washington, D.C.

1988 Massachusetts Artists Fellowship (finalist)

Artist in Residence, Light Work, Syracuse, N.Y.

1989 Massachusetts Artists Fellowship (finalist)

1989–90 Artists in Residence, Rhode Island School of Design, Providence, R.I.

1990 Artists in Residence, Art Institute of Chicago

Artists in Residence, Rhode Island School of Design

1991 NEFA/NEA photography Fellowship Exhibition, Mills College Art Gallery, Oakland, Calif.

1992 Louis Comfort Tiffany Award

1993–94 Artist in Residence, Cité des Arts, Paris, France

National Endowment for the Arts Fellowship

"Photographer of the Year," awarded by the Friends of Photography, Ansel Adams Center, San Francisco, Calif.

1994–95 National Endowment for the Arts Visual Arts Grant

1995 The May Ingraham Bunting Award, Radcliffe College, Cambridge, Mass.

1996 The Alpert Award for Visual Arts

1997–98 Philip Morris Resident, Künstlerhaus Bethanien, Berlin, Germany

SELECTED BIBLIOGRAPHY

1981

Weems, Carrie Mae. *Blues & Pinks*. Artist's book, 1981.

1982

Doniger, Sidney, Sandra Matthews, and Gillian Brown, eds. "Personal Perspectives on the Evolution of American Black Photography: A Talk with Carrie Weems." *Obscura*: 2, 4 (Spring 1982): 8–17.

Weems, Carrie Mae. *Stories*. Artist's book, 1982.

———. *Vanishing Cream*. Artist's book, 1982.

1984

Weems, Carrie Mae. *Family Pictures and Stories: A Photographic Installation*. San Diego, Calif.: Alternative Space Gallery, 1984.

1985

Tamblyn, Christine. "Three Views of Families." *Artweek*, 26 October 1985, 11.

1987

Hall, Stuart. "Minimal Selves." *ICA Document 6: Identity*. London: ICA, 1987.

Ollman, Leah. "At The Galleries." *Los Angeles Times* (San Diego County), 16 October 1987, Part VI, 26B.

1988

Freeland, Cynthia. *The Other*. Houston, Tex.: Houston Center for Photography, 1988.

Mellor, Carl. "No Joke: Photographer Carrie Mae Weems Blasts Away Stereotypes." *Syracuse New Times*, 31 August–7 September 1988, 1+.

Wallis, Brian. "Questioning Documentary." *Aperture* 112 (Fall 1988): 60–71.

Weems, Carrie Mae. Statement in *Edict and Episode: Meaning and Image*. San Diego, Calif.: Installation Gallery, 1988.

1989

Levinson, Nan. "M.I.T. exhibit goes beyond just throwing art at problems." *In These Times*, 13–16 December 1989, 18.

Rosenthal, Mel. "Commentary." *Nueva Luz 2*, 22–32. New York: En Foco, 1989.

Willis-Thomas, Deborah, and Howard Dodson. *Black Photographers Bear Witness: 100 Years of Social Protest*. Willamstown, Mass.: Willams College Museum of Art, 1989.

Wilson, Judith. "Stereotypes, Or a Picture Is Worth a Thousand Lies." In *Prisoners of Image: Ethnic and Gender Stereotypes*. New York: Alternative Museum, 1989.

1990

Carrie Mae Weems. Washington, D.C.: National Museum of Women in the Arts, 1990.

"Disputed Identities." *SF Camerawork* 17, 3 (Fall 1990): 7, 29

Signs of the Self: Changing Perceptions. Woodstock, N.Y.: Woodstock Artists Association, 1990.

Aletti, Vince. "Choices." *The Village Voice,* 30 October 1990, 105.

Gibbs, Michael. "Critical Realism." *Perspektief* 39 (1990): 38–58.

Jackson, Wendy. "Mixed Mesages." *Hartford Advocate,* 12 November 1990, 14.

Jones, Kellie. "In Their Own Image." *Artforum 29,* no. 3 (November 1990): 133–38.

Schwendenwien, Jude. "A Look at Privilege, Presumption." *Hartford Courant,* 18 November 1990, G6.

Sherlock, Maureen P. "A Dangerous Age: The Midlife Crisis of Postmodern Feminism." *Arts Magazine* 65, no. 1 (September 1990): 17–74.

van Cook, Marguerite. "Carrie Mae Weems: The Right Questions." *Village Beat,* December 1990, 12.

Weems, Carrie Mae. *And 22 Million Very Tired and Very Angry People.* San Francisco, Calif.: Walter/McBean Gallery, San Francisco Art Institute, 1990.

———. "Making Art, Making Money: 13 Artists Comment." *Art in America* 78, no. 7 (July 1990): 140.

———. "THEN WHAT? Photographs and Folklore." Buffalo, N.Y.: CEPA Gallery, 1990.

1991

"Carrie Mae Weems/Matrix 115, Wadsworth Atheneum." *Journal of the Print World* 14, no. 2 (Spring 1991): 49.

Family Pictures and Stories: A Photographic Installation. Reading, Pa.: Albright College Freedman Gallery, Center for the Arts, 1991.

"Interview." *Atelier* (January 1991): 35–37.

"A Portrait Is Not a Likeness." *The Archive,* no. 29 (1991).

1991 Biennial Exhibition. New York, N.Y.: Whitney Museum of American Art, 1991.

Buck, Louisa. "Balance or Baggage? Whitney Biennial." *Women's Art Magazine* 41 (July/August, 1991): 18–19.

Coleman, Sandy. "A Family Album on Exhibit." *The Boston Globe,* 10 November 1991, sec. 11, 1.

Curtis, Cathy. "Down-Home Look Belies Power of Carrie Mae Weems's Work." *Los Angeles Times* (Orange County), 21 October 1991, F3.

Dowd, Maureen. "Yes, but Can She Make Them Swoon." *The New York Times,* 26 May 1991, E6.

Felshin, Nina. *No Laughing Matter.* New York: Independent Curators Incorporated, 1991.

Galassi, Peter. *The Pleasures and Terrors of Domestic Comfort.* New York: Museum of Modern Art, 1991.

Heartney, Eleanor. "Carrie Mae Weems." *ARTnews* 90, 1 (January 1991): 154–55.

Johnson, Ken. "Report from New York: The Whitney's Generational Saga." *Art in America* 79, 6 (June 1991): 45–51.

Littlefield, Kinney. "Photography and Poetry Extract Beauty from Pain." *Orange County Register,* 25 October 1991, 48.

Miller, Donald. "PCA photo show sharp." *Pittsburgh Post-Gazette,* 27 April 1991, 10.

Miller-Keller, Andrea. *Carrie Mae Weems/MATRIX 115.* Hartford, Conn.: Wadsworth Atheneum, 1991.

Moore, Catriona. "The Art of Political Correctness." *Art & Text,* 41 (1991): 32–39.

Nesbit, Perry. *Family Picture and Stories: A Photographic Installation.* Reading, Pa.: Freedman Gallery, Albright College, 1991.

Plagens, Peter. "A House Is Not a Home." *Newsweek,* 21 October 1991, 62–63.

Princethal, Nancy. "Carrie Mae Weems at P.P.O.W." *Art in America* 79, 1 (January 1991): 129.

Reid, Calvin. "A Dangerous Age: The Mid-Life Crisis of Postmodern Feminism." *Art Magazine* (January 1991): 70.

Rodriguez, Geno. *Artists of Conscience: 16 Years of Social and Political Commentary*. New York: Alternative Museum, 1991.

Scott, Martha B. *The Art of Advocacy*. Ridgefield, Conn.: Aldrich Museum of Contemporary Art, 1991.

Siegel, Jeanne. "The 1991 Whitney Biennial." *Tema Celeste* (May/June 1991): 97.

Squire, Carol. "Domestic Blitz: The Modern Cleans House." *Artforum* 30, 2 (October 1991): 88–91.

Tarlow, Lois. "Carrie Mae Weems." *Art New England* 12 (August/September 1991): Cover + 10–12.

Tippi, Laura. *And 22 Million Very Tired and Very Angry People*. New York: New Museum of Contemporary Art, 1991.

Wrigh, Erin. "Trustman House Exceptional Exhibit." *The Simmons News* (14 February 1991): 8.

1992

And 22 Million Very Tired and Very Angry People. San Fransisco, Calif.: Walter/McBean Gallery, San Francisco Art Institute, 1992.

"Portraits of Pride: Black Family Life in America." *The Boston Globe,* 6 January 1992, sec 34, 4.

Schwarze Kunst Konzepte zur Politik und Identität. Berlin: Neue Gesellschaft für Bildende Kunst, 1992.

Aletti, Vince. "Dark Passage." *The Village Voice,* 22 December 1992, 102–103.

Barnard, Elissa. "American Activist Art No Laughing Matter." *The Mail Star,* 6 March 1992, C8.

Benner, Susan. "A Conversation with Carrie Mae Weems." *Art Week* 23 (7 May 1992): 4–5.

Bricker Balken, Debra. "Carrie Mae Weems at P.P.O.W." *Art in America* (April 1992): 129–30.

Coleman, A. D. "Cultural Tenacity Among the Gullah." *The New York Observer,* 21 December 1992, 14.

Hagen, Charles. "Gullah Culture Casts Its Spell." *The New York Times,* 27 November 1992, C1, C22.

Hess, Elizabeth. "Dirty Laundry." *The Village Voice,* 12 May 1992, 91.

Liebowitz, Herbert. "Parnassus: Poetry in Review." *Poetry in Review* 17, 1 (1992), cover.

Kelley, Jeff. "The Isms Brothers: Carrie Mae Weems at SFAI." *Art Week* 23 (7 May 1992): 4.

MacDonald, Cathy. "Frighteningly Funny." *Daily News* (Nova Scotia), 5 March 1992.

Moore, Catrions. "The Art of Political Correctness." *Art & Text,* Volume 41 (1992): 32–39.

Phillips, Patricia C. "Public Art: The Point in Between." *Sculpture* 2, 3 (May/June 1992): 37–41.

Saunders, Charles. "No Laughing Matter." *The Daily News, Sunday Perspective,* 12 April 1992.

Slavin, Jeri. *Center Margins*. Fredonia, N.Y.: Michael C. Rockefeller Arts Center, State University College, Fredonia, 1992.

Stanley, Sherry M., M.D. *Parents*. Dayton, Ohio: Dayton Art Institute Museum of Contemporary Art, Creative Arts Center, Wright State University, 1992.

Stevens, Mitchell. "A Family Affair." *New Art Examiner* (May 1992): 17.

Wise, Kelly. "Exhibit Spotlight Contemporary Artists." *The Boston Globe,* 8 February 1992, 16.

1993

"A Question of Color." *The San Francisco Examiner,* 6 June 1993, 29.

"Grappling with Feminism and Femininity." *The New York Times,* 11 March 1993, 22.

"New Acquisitions." *Santa Barbara Museum of Art Bulletin* (May/June 1993): 4.

Becker, Jochen. "Mis/Taken Identities." *Kunstforum* 123 (1993): 320.

Behr, Martin. "Ist Rassismus ein Sehfehler? Mit Fotos auf Identitaetssuche." *Salzburger Nachrichten,* 7 May 1993.

Bonetti, David. "A Question of Colors." *The San Francisco Examiner,* 6 June 1993, 29.

Bonetti, David. "Looking Truth in the Face. Carrie Mae Weems Delivers Political Messages with Human Spirit." *The San Francisco Examiner,* 18 June 1993, E7.

Braff, Phylis. "How Artists' Creations Relate to Society." *The New York Times,* 2 May 1993, LI-24.

Foerstner, Abigail. "Take a Spring Stroll to 4 River North Galleries." *The Chicago Tribune,* 30 April 1993, 7, 89.

Hamilton, David. "Carrie Mae Weems: Indictments of Racism in Black and White." *Art and Antiques* (September 1993): 89.

Heartney, Eleanor. "Carrie Mae Weems at P.P.O.W." *ARTnews* (February 1993): 109.

Henry, Gerrit. "Books in Review." *The Print Collector's Newsletter* (September/October, 1993): 153.

Kirsh, Andrea, and Susan Fisher Sterling. *Carrie Mae Weems.* Washington, D.C.: The National Museum of Women in the Arts, 1993.

Lewis, Jo Ann. "Lessons in the Stories: The Engaging Voice of Carrie Mae Weems." *The Washington Post,* 7 January 1993, C2.

Linker, Kate. "Went Looking for Africa." *Artforum,* 31, 6 (February 1993): 79–82.

McKenna, Kristine. "The Evolution of a Tough Cookie." *The Los Angeles Times,* Calendar, 27 June 1993, 4.

Patterson, Tom. "Photograph Exhibit at SECCA Focuses on African-American Life." *Winston-Salem Journal,* 19 December 1993, C3.

Raynor, Vivien. "A Multicultural Mosaic and Postcards from the Urban Edge." *The New York Times,* 26 December 1993, 16.

———. "Grappling with Feminism and Feminity." *The New York Times,* 11 March 1993, 22.

Rich, Ruby. "Weems's World." *Mirabella* (February 1993): 44–45.

Richardson, Trevor. "Fictions of the Self: A Portrait of Contemporary Photography." Greensboro, N.C.: Weatherspoon Art Gallery, The University of North Carolina, 1993.

1994

Baker, Houston A. Jr. *In these Islands: South Carolina, Georgia.* Tuscaloosa, Ala.: Sarah Moody Gallery of Art, University of Alabama, 1994.

Golden, Thelma. *Black Male, Representations of Masculinity in Contemporary American Art.* New York, N.Y.: The Whitney Museum of American Art/Harry N. Abrams, 1994.

Griffin, Farah Jasmine, and Tobing Rony. *Personal Narrative: Women Photographers of Color.* Winston-Salem, N.C.: Southeastern Center for Contemporary Art, 1994.

Jacob, Mary Jane. *Carrie Mae Weems*. Philadelphia, Pa.: The Fabric Workshop/Museum, 1994.

Kimmelman, Michael. "Black Male." *The New York Times,* 11 November 1994.

Sozanski, Edward. "An Empathetic View of History and Family." *The Philadelphia Inquirer,* 9 December 1994.

1995

"Carrie Mae Weems to Create Installation Exploring Representation of African Americans in Photography." *Los Angeles Bay News,* 23 February 1995.

Anderson, Michael. "Review." *ArtIssues* (Summer 1995): 42.

Bonetti, David. "Visual History of African America." *The San Francisco Examiner,* 9 May 1995, C3.

Frank, Peter. "Art Picks of the Week: Carrie Mae Weems, Charles Gaines, Noah Purifoy." *LA Weekly,* 9–15 June 1995.

hooks, bell. "Talking Art with Carrie Mae Weems." In *Art on My Mind: Visual Politics,* 74–93. New York: The New Press, 1995.

Salpeter, Ellen F., Anne R. Pasternak, and Herbert Muschamp. "If They Built a Memorial to the War in the Streets: Seven Proposals to Honor the Urban Dead." *The New York Times Magazine* (9 April 1995): 56–61.

Schmerler, Sarah. "Review." *Time Out,* 22–29 November 1995, 25.

Skvirsky, Karina, and Jennifer Pearson. *Art About Life: Contemporary American Culture*. Bloomington: Fine Arts Gallery, Indiana University, 1995.

Smith, Roberta. "A Photographer Upstages Herself." *The New York Times,* 22 December 1995, C31.

1996

Burning Issues: Contemporary African-American Art. Fort Lauderdale, Fla.: Museum of Art, 1996.

Aletti, Vince. "Review." *The Village Voice,* 30 January 1996.

Canning, Susan. "Review." *Art Papers,* 20, 2 (March/April, 1996): 50.

Halle, Howard. "Review." *Time Out,* 24–31 January 1996, 26.

Johnson, Patricia J. "Balance the Table." *The Houston Chronicle,* 8 April 1996.

Neumaier, Diane. *Reframings: New American Feminist Photographies*. Philadelphia: Temple University Press, 1996.

Sichel, Berta. "Carrie Mae Weems retrata a disápora negra." *Terca-Feira* (São Paulo, Brazil), 6 February 1996, D8.

Soutter, Lucy. "By Any Means Necessary: Document and Fiction in the Work of Carrie Mae Weems." *Art & Design Profile No. 51* (1996): 70–75.

Turner, Grady T. "Review." *Art in America* (June, 1996): 103.

1997

Dislocations. Finland: Rovaniemi Art Museum/HarperCollins Publishers, 1997.

Original Visions, Shifting the Paradigm, Women's Art 1970–1996. Boston, Mass.: McMullen Museum of Art, Boston College, 1997.

Armitage, Diane. "Review." *THE Magazine* (May 1997): 39.

Berkovitch, Ellen. "Documentary or Fiction? Photographer Establishes Scenes, Then Exits." *Journal North,* 10 April 1997, 4.

Chandler, Mary Voelz. "Artists exhibit visual autobiographies." *Rocky Mountain News,* 14 September 1997, D16.

Hofstadter, Dan. "A Parade of Immigrants Passing Before the Lens." *The New York Times,* 16 May 1997, C1.

Jackson, Phyllis J. "(In)Forming the Visual: (Re)presenting Women of African Descent." *The International Review of African-American Art,* 14, 3 (1997): 31.

Joselit, David. "Exhibiting Gender." *Art in America* (January 1997): 36–39.

McCloud, Kathleen. "Twist and Turn of Truth." *Pasatiempo,* 4 April 1997, 42.

Roland, Marya. "Tragic Wake...." *Art Papers* (March/April 1997): 68.

Powell, Richard J. *Black Art and Culture in the 20th Century*. London: Thames & Hudson, 1997.

Weibel, Peter. *Inclusion/Exclusion*. Austria: DuMont Bücherverlag, 1997.

1998

Johnson, Ken. "Review." *The New York Times,* 22 May 1998, E35.

Kashara, Michiko. *The Politics Behind the Nude*. Tokyo: Chikuma Shobo Publishing Co., 1998.

Kimmelman, Michael. "When a Glint in the Eye Showed Crime in the Genes." *The New York Times,* 22 May 1998, E31.